SISKIYOU COUNTY LIBRARY

3 2871 00289849 8

D0961292

A New Owner's
Guide to
COCKER SPANIELS

JG-106

Overleaf: Adult and puppy Cocker Spaniels owned by April Stitch.

Opposite Page: Cocker Spaniel owned by Carolee Douglas.

The Publisher wishes to acknowledge the following owners of the dogs in this book: Mary and David Adams, Ruth Baumgartner, Brad and Brigitte Berg, Pat and Dan Brannan, Nona Burrell, Catherine L. Carey, Shirley Collier, Rita Crowe, Diane Donnelly, Carolee Douglas, Geraldine Drayer, Joy Farlow, Barbara J. Hoops, Judith P. Iby, Trish Jackson, Mike Kinchsular, David Kittredge, Fronci Knifong, Roberta Kohl, Patti Kunkle, Barbara Marsh, Jane Mohr, Sam and Wilma Parker, Carole Paul, Sharon D. Reed, April Stich, Tina Turner.

Photographers: Alverson Photographers, Inc., Ashbey Photography, Booth Photography, Paulette Braun, Catherine L. Carey, Wayne Cott, Isabelle Francais, Judith P. Iby, Merck AgVet, Paul's, Robert Pearcy, Photo by Phoebe, Vince Serbin, Skeeters, Judith E. Strom, Karen Taylor.

© 1996 by T.F.H. Publications, Inc.

Distributed in the UNITED STATES to the Pet Trade by T.F.H. Publications, Inc., One T.F.H. Plaza, Neptune City, NJ 07753; distributed in the UNITED STATES to the Bookstore and Library Trade by National Book Network, Inc. 4720 Boston Way, Lanham MD 20706; in CANADA to the Pet Trade by H & L Pet Supplies Inc., 27 Kingston Crescent, Kitchener, Ontario N2B 2T6; Rolf C. Hagen Inc., 3225 Sartelon St. Laurent-Montreal Quebec H4R 1E8; in CANADA to the Book Trade by Vanwell Publishing Ltd., 1 Northrup Crescent, St. Catharines, Ontario L2M 6P5 ; in ENGLAND by T.F.H. Publications, PO Box 15, Waterlooville PO7 6BQ; in AUSTRALIA AND THE SOUTH PACIFIC by T.F.H. (Australia), Pty. Ltd., Box 149, Brookvale 2100 N.S.W., Australia; in NEW ZEALAND by Brooklands Aquarium Ltd. 5 McGiven Drive, New Plymouth, RD1 New Zealand; in Japan by T.F.H. Publications, Japan— Jiro Tsuda, 10-12-3 Ohjidai, Sakura, Chiba 285, Japan; in SOUTH AFRICA by Lopis (Pty) Ltd., P.O. Box 39127, Booysens, 2016, Johannesburg, South Africa. Published by T.F.H. Publications, Inc.

MANUFACTURED IN THE UNITED STATES OF AMERICA BY T.F.H. PUBLICATIONS, INC.

636.752

498

A New Owner's Guide to Cocker Spaniels

Judith P. Iby

SISKIYOU COUNTY PUBLIC LIBRARY
719 FOURTH STREET
YREKA, CALIFORNIA 96097

Contents

Choosing a Cocker Spaniel puppy from this adorable trio is no easy task.

Cocker Spaniel puppies should be alert, displaying bright eyes and a shiny, wet nose.

The Cocker Spaniel is the smallest member of the Sporting Group.

Urination · Clean Ups · Fenced-In Yard · Being a Good Neighbor · Equipment · Exercise

The Cocker Spaniel is a natural hunter and retriever, both on land and in the water.

Cockers love to jump and do well in obedience trials and the like.

DEDICATION

I dedicate this book to Cocker Spaniels, who give so much and ask so little, and to their owners around the world. I also dedicate this book to my wonderful dogs who have so patiently watched me write it.

The love and devotion between the author and the Cocker Spaniels in her life is apparent.

ACKNOWLEDGMENTS

The author is grateful to the following veterinarians for their contributions and assistance in writing the health sections of this book: Dr. Kerry L. Ketring, DACVO, All Animal Eye Clinic, Cincinnati; Dr. John Gordon, American College of Veterinary Dermatology, MEDVET, Columbus; Dr. Kevin D. Ketring and Dr. Joseph P. Stratman, College Hill Pet Clinic, Cincinnati. A special thank you to Wilma Parker for her unfailing support.

Ch. Sandor's Settin' The Pace, UDT, owned by the author practicing the bar jump for Utility.

HISTORY of the Cocker Spaniel

The Cocker Spaniel has a truly fascinating history. As long ago as the late 1300s the "Spaynell" was mentioned in Geoffrey Chaucer's writings. Did you perhaps study Shakespeare and recall spaniels in his plays? Even though he was not a dog lover, he included them in at least nine plays. That certainly was a long time ago, the late 1500s, and surely lends itself to an illustrious past for our spaniels.

The noble Cocker Spaniel has an illustrious past, dating back as early as the 1500s.

Would you be surprised to learn that one of the two dogs who sailed on the Mayflower in 1620 was a Spaniel? The other was a Mastiff. I surmise that the Mastiff was an excellent guard dog, defending the Pilgrims against the Indians, and was also adept at bringing home deer and other large game. There is no doubt that the spaniel with his keen nose and cleverness excelled at hunting the smaller game. Presumably these dogs mated with the dogs already present in North America. Later, other dogs, including different breeds, arrived with the new settlers.

There are drawings of dogs on cave walls as early as 11000 B.C. in Altamira, Spain and Lascaux, France. During this era, dogs hunted many types of game, including

One of the two dogs who sailed on the Mayflower in 1620 was a spaniel; however, it is impossible to trace today's Cocker Spaniels' descent from this dog.

bison, deer, wild horses and of course small game. Those first dogs primarily hunted large game. As you can well imagine, a good hunting dog may have determined whether there was dinner that day. Around 6000 B.C., Sheepdogs were bred to guard and herd the flocks. Eventually, when life became more civilized, the smaller dogs became popular.

The name spaniel originated from the word "Hispania," which was the old name for Spain. Not only did spaniels originate from and develop in Spain but they also developed in France and England. Centuries later they were to become the most popular breed in England and America.

I am sure your friends who own Pointers, Flat-Coated Retrievers and Labradors would be surprised to learn that spaniels are way back in their dogs' ancestries. Flat-Coated and Curly-Coated Retrievers descend from a spaniel/setter cross and Labradors were

Our present-day Cocker Spaniels still wear the vibrant colors of the toy spaniels, as shown by these gorgeous Parti-colors.

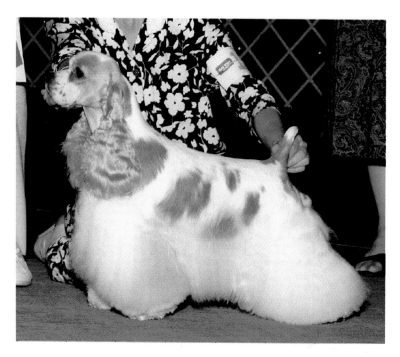

According to English history, the Parti-color Cocker Spaniels were the most popular colors and are still among the favorite today.

originally bred from spaniels and Newfoundlands. Of course, most breeds descend from a combination of several different breeds.

EARLY HUNTING

Spaniels proved to be great hunters, working both on land and in the water. Customarily they ran in front of their masters, quartering the ground and scenting and raising fowl, such as partridge and quail. They also acted as "crouchers," downing to the ground in front of the game, which enabled the fowl to be taken with a net. Hawks hovered above the game which encouraged the fowl to stay close to the ground while the hunters covered the area with the net and captured the game. During that era, gun loading was quite time consuming so the net was needed to keep the game from escaping. In this day and age that doesn't seem quite fair, but we must

Dog showing began in 1859 in England and in 1874 in the United States and has grown tremendously ever since. Here Ch. Rendition Triple Play is making history. remember that game was an important food source. Not only were Spaniels good on land, but they excelled as swimmers and in retrieving ducks from the water. Cockers derived their name from their adeptness at hunting woodcock.

In the years to come, Spaniels were bred as pets for ladies, sporting dogs for sportsmen and eventually as show dogs. They have excelled in all those capacities and are no longer lady's dogs but man's dogs as well! There is nothing delicate about the breed. Their sporting instincts and sturdy structure enable them to do it all—hunt, show, and be faithful, loving companion dogs.

Breed Evolution

During those early spaniel years the breed was diversified in type compared to the many present-day spaniel breeds. Later the spaniel was divided into two groups: land spaniels and water spaniels. Toy spaniels, the Cockers (English and American), the Sussex and the Springers (Welsh and English) comprised the land group. The water group included the Irish Water Spaniel and the American Water Spaniel.

The toy spaniels were also called pet spaniels because of their small size. These delightful little dogs consisted of the English Toy Spaniel, the Cavalier King Charles Spaniel, the black and white Dutch Spaniel, and the Red and White Italian Spaniel. Our present-day Cockers still wear the vibrant colors of the toy spaniels.

During the early 1900s tri-colors were not readily accepted; however, today these lovely colors are in demand by show and pet homes.

Early Dog Showing and Registration

Even though a spaniel sailed the Mayflower, it is impossible to trace our American Cocker's descent from this dog since our AKC Stud Book was not formed until the 1800s. In 1879 the first Cocker, a liver and white named Captain, was registered with the National American Kennel Club, which eventually became the American Kennel Club.

A wonderful sport began in England in 1859—dog showing! June of 1874 was the beginning of dog shows in America and the sport has grown tremendously. The Kennel Club of England was formed in 1859 and the American Kennel Club followed in 1884. Around 1870 the Cockers and Springers of the land spaniel group became Field Spaniels. At that time they were divided by weight (under 25 pounds and over 25 pounds) and depending on their weight they became Field or Cocker Spaniels, the former being the heavier. Littermates could be registered as different varieties depending on their weight. I wonder how they went about registering them since I assume they would have to wait on their weight. Interesting!

The first order of business for the newly formed American Spaniel Club in 1891 was to separate the Cockers from the Field Spaniels. The main criteria was again weight and if the dog weighed over 28 pounds it automatically became a Field Spaniel. Occasionally such a dog would be shown in the Cocker class at a show and frequently was weighed. If the

In the late 1800s solid black Cocker Spaniels were hard to find. A black Field Spaniel named Benedict is to thank for the surge in black Cockers around this time in America.

dog was over the allowed weight then it was promptly removed from the class. The weight limitation for Cockers was replaced by height limitations in 1943. During this era, as well as today, the differences between the breeds (besides the weight) were height and length of body. The American Kennel Club separated the Cocker and Field Spaniels in 1905 but this was already accomplished in 1893 with the English Kennel Club.

Today's Cocker evolved from a "new look" that was created in the 1940s, bringing forth an even taller Cocker, more compact with a slope to the topline and a higher tailset.

SEPARATION OF ENGLISH AND AMERICAN COCKERS

It wasn't until 1946 that the English Cockers received their own identity, largely through the efforts of Mrs. Geraldine Rockefeller Dodge. The Cocker Spaniel and English Cocker had grown further apart after the first World War, the latter being somewhat larger, rangier, and narrower in the chest, with a longer and narrower head. The Cocker breeders were developing a smaller, shorter-backed dog with a more domed head. The muzzle was also shorter and fuller. In addition, the Cocker Spaniel's coat is more plush than its cousin, the English Cocker.

THE NAME

In America the name Cocker Spaniel stands for the American Cocker Spaniel but in other countries the name would denote the English Cocker. A few years ago the American Spaniel Club membership was polled regarding changing the name Cocker to American Cocker but the membership elected to keep Cocker Spaniel.

The American Spaniel Club originated in 1891 and remains the national club for the breed today.

THE THREE VARIETIES

At one time there were four varieties—the English variety, Parti-color, Black, and ASCOB (**A**ny **S**olid **C**olor **O**ther than **B**lack). Originally the English, Parti-color and Black prevailed but the ASCOB variety earned recognition in the early '40s. After separation of the English and Cocker Spaniels only the three varieties reigned.

The black and tans were originally shown with the Parti-colors, then were shifted to the ASCOB variety and finally moved to the Black variety where they are shown today. The black and tans had to struggle for acceptance even though the first Cockers shown in this country were black and tans. During this era the tri-colors were not readily accepted, but today these lovely colors are in demand by show and pet homes.

Actually the Parti-colors (black/whites, red/whites, and liver/whites) were the most popular colors according to English history. Solid blacks were hard to find. American

history from 1882 talks about the 40-pound black Field Spaniel, Benedict, that showed at Westminster Kennel Club. A new era was to begin

It wasn't until 1946 that the English Cocker (shown here) received its own identity.

RESERVE
WINNERS

AMERICAN
SPANIEL CLUB
JANUARY
1991
DAVE ASHBEY

because all the breeders bred to him. History goes on to say that it took several generations to get the type of dog they desired, but they did get black!

Brown and tan Cocker Spaniels are included in the ASCOB variety.

OBO TYPE

Ch. Obo was whelped in 1879 and was the common ancestor of both the English and the American Cocker. His son, Ch. Obo II, became the progenitor of Cocker Spaniels. Obo II's dam was Ch. Chloe II who was bred to Ch. Obo before being shipped to America. Obo II was a great dog in his day but barely resembled the Cocker today. He was 10 inches tall at the withers and was 29 inches from his nose to the root of his tail.

It is obvious that conformation in those days was greatly different from Cocker type today. The old type (Obo type) was long in body, low on leg (about 9 or 10 inches from foot to withers compared to about 14 to 15 inches today), moderate in muzzle and head (coarse compared to our finely chiseled heads today) and scant feathering covering only the back of the legs and the underbody.

THE "NEW LOOK"

Today's Cocker type evolved from the "new look" created in the '30s and '40s. In the '30s the Cocker was higher on leg, more compact and shorter in the muzzle. The pattern

The black and tan Cocker Spaniels were originally exhibited with the Parti-colors and were then shifted to the ASCOB variety and finally moved to the Black variety where they are shown today.

of feathering had not changed. The '40s brought forth an even taller Cocker, more compact with a slope to the topline and a higher tailset. It wore a heavier coat with good feathering, covering the entire leg and sides and under the body. Our modern Cockers wear this same look and are probably just a little bit more elegant.

THE FAMOUS FROM YEARS AGO

One of our very most famous Cockers was Ch. My Own Brucie owned by Mr. Herbert Mellenthin from Poughkeepsie, NY. My Own Brucie captured many, many hearts when he won back-to-back Best in Shows at Westminster Kennel Club ("the Garden") in 1940 and 1941. My Own Brucie, a Red Brucie son, was always shown by his owner. It is said they were inseparable. Rumor goes that My Own Brucie was sold for $10,000 to Mr. and Mrs. Peter Garvan upon the death of his owner. Even though he received excellent care from the Garvans he died prematurely at the age of eight. His obituary was published on the front page of the *New York Evening Sun.*

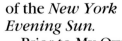

Cocker Spaniels at the end of the 18th century were moderate in muzzle and head, appearing coarse compared to our finely chiseled heads today.

Prior to My Own Brucie's claim to fame another Cocker won BIS at Westminster in 1921, Ch. Midkiff Seductive, a black and white bitch owned by William T. Payne who was influential in changing attitudes toward color. Many of our Partis are descended from her great-great grandparents. Only one other Cocker has achieved a Best in Show win at Westminster Kennel Club, Ch. Camor's Rise and Shine shown by the late Ted Young, Jr. and owned by Mrs. Carl Morgan. This prestigious win occurred in 1954.

Back to the William Payne era. Would you believe that Mr. Payne owned 350 Cockers that ran loose on his 30-acre farm when they weren't kenneled? Another distinguished gentleman, Mr. O.B. Gilman acquired the Idahurst Kennel in the early 1900s. His kennel was equipped to house 125 adult Cockers and puppies. Also there were facilities for 24 bitches whelping simultaneously. This is unbelievable by today's standards where we promote better quality out

Over the years breeders have worked diligently at improving the temperament, conformation and quality of health of their Cocker puppies.

of fewer litters with emphasis on socialization and good homes. However, during those days raising dogs was not only a hobby but a business. Large breeders such as Mr. Payne and Mr. Gilman employed kennel managers and assistants. Frequently the kennel manager was responsible or partly responsible for planning the breedings.

When you think of it, Cockers had to be a hardy breed to have survived. Are you aware there was no vaccine for distemper until the virus was confirmed during the period of 1926-1928. Dogs dropped like flies and if they lived, they showed signs of neurological problems. Heartworm disease was present, but there was no preventative and few checked for it unless the dog was sick. When you read of treatments for skin problems, parasites and other common ailments, you wonder how they survived. In those days the diets left much to be desired since dogs were fed table scraps, raw meat and a concoction of other foods. Dog food manufacturing and research hadn't come into its own.

WHERE ARE WE TODAY?

The Cocker Spaniel has been listed in the top ten AKC registrations since prior to 1936 at which time it climbed to the number one spot. It remained in this position (for 17 years) until 1953 when the Beagle took over. During its peak it reached 78,501, which totaled 30 percent of the entire AKC registrations. In contrast the Cocker was still within the top ten registrations in 1994 but only 60,888 were registered.

The Cocker boom of the '40s nearly wrecked the breed. Any breed that becomes popular is likely to suffer the consequences of indiscriminate and haphazard breeding. As a whole, AKC registrations are down, which is probably in response to the limited registration that is now available. Breeders requested this type of registration to prevent indiscriminate breeding of their offspring. This should encourage more responsible breeding.

Today's Cocker Spaniel breeders promote better quality out of fewer litters. All six of these nine-month-old littermates have finished their championships.

Gone are the large kennels and large breeding programs. It is no longer a business, but a hobby. Over the years breeders have diligently worked at improving temperament, conformation and the quality of health. There are many, many famous Cockers today that are excelling in conformation, obedience, agility, hunting and last but not least as good producers.

There are many Cocker Spaniels that excel in dog sports, such as agility. This Cocker flies over the bar jump at an agility trial.

Cocker Spaniels are hunting dogs by nature. This is Ch. Magic Makers T.J. Madison, CD, TD, WDX, JH, SH, showing off his prize.

Regardless of whether it is winning Best in Show or the family companion dog, the Cocker Spaniel is surely loved and has retained its popularity.

STANDARD for the Cocker Spaniel

L isted below are some of the highlights of the American Spaniel Club Standard for the Cocker Spaniel.

GENERAL APPEARANCE

The Cocker Spaniel is the smallest member of the Sporting Group. He has a sturdy compact body and a cleanly chiseled and refined head, with the overall dog in complete balance and of ideal size. He stands well up at the shoulder on straight forelegs with a topline sloping slightly toward strong, moderately bent, muscular quarters. He is a dog capable of considerable speed combined with great endurance. Above all, he must be free and merry, sound, well-balanced throughout, and in action show a keen inclination to work. A dog well balanced in all parts is more desirable than a dog with strongly contrasting good points and faults.

VARIETIES

Cocker Spaniels come in a variety of colors and are classified by color into three varieties. At a dog show the winner of each variety competes in the Sporting Group. The three varieties are Black, ASCOB (**A**ny **S**olid **C**olor **O**ther than **B**lack) and Parti-color. The Black variety includes black and black and tan and the ASCOB variety includes all shades of buff (from silver to deepest red), brown and brown and tan. A small amount of white is allowed on the chest of the blacks and the ASCOBs. The Partis include a rainbow of colors, which include black/tan/white and brown/tan/white. These are the most common colors. There are a few breeders breeding for the roan colors, which would be comparable to the English Cocker roan colors.

There are some lovely sable and sable/white Cockers that are eligible for AKC registration but are unacceptable according to the American Spaniel Club Standard and therefore are not showable. Unfortunately some sellers inflate their prices for these less common colors.

In order to show a black/tan or brown/tan, the tan points are restricted to less than 10% of the color and are to be clearly visible as follows:

1. A clear spot over each eye;
2. On the sides of the muzzle and on the cheeks;
3. On the underside of the ears;
4. On all feet and/or legs;
5. Under the tail;
6. On the chest, optional; presence or absence shall not be penalized.

A promising Cocker Spaniel pup can be anything that you desire: a champion, companion dog, therapy dog, and more—but definitely a best friend!

In my opinion, the Parti-colors are the hardest to breed and show because of their spots. The location of the spots can enhance or ruin a show dog. There are to be two or more solid, well-broken colors, one of

which must be white and the other to be red, black or brown, and roans, and can include any such color combination with tan points. It is preferable that the tan markings be located in the same pattern as for the tan points in the Black and ASCOB varieties. Roans are classified as Parti-colors and may be of any of the usual roaning patterns. Primary color that is 90% or more shall disqualify.

COAT

Our Standard states that an excessive, curly or cottony coat is to be penalized. A silky, flat or slightly wavy coat is to be desired. Many admire the Cocker's profuse coat but it does require care. When you are looking at a puppy, consider the coat and its texture and try to see the coat on the parents. This should give you an idea of what to expect. Experienced breeders know how to care for it but pet owners may be stymied and don't want the hassle. Frequently they keep their Cockers shaved down, which is truly a shame but better than letting them get severely matted. Other pet owners keep their Cockers in "puppy" trims. The truly dedicated keep up with the Cocker's long and flowing coat. There is nothing prettier than a well-kept Cocker in full coat.

Many quality puppies are placed in pet homes because they are lacking enough coat to make it as a show dog. Keep in mind that the coat grows more profusely after spaying and neutering. Also some very good puppies don't make the grade as show

The tan points on black and tan Cocker Spaniels should be located over each eye, on the sides of the muzzle, on the underside of the ears, on all feet and/or legs, and under the tail.

This Parti-color Cocker (brown and white) displays beautiful markings and conformation. Notice how she holds her tail up.

candidates because of their color, lack of or too much, and/or in the wrong places.

HEAD

The Cocker Spaniel is probably best known for its beautifully chiseled head. The skull should be rounded with no tendency towards flatness. The eyeballs are round and full and look directly forward and the eye rims give a slightly almond-shaped appearance. The color of the iris is dark brown, the darker the better. The red/white liver-nosed Partis do not carry the pigment for brown eyes and have greenish-colored eyes. Point of interest: the browns and brown/whites have blue eyes as puppies that change to green and eventually to brown, which may not occur till about five to six months of age.

The ears are to be placed no higher than a line to the lower part of the eye and are to be well feathered. The muzzle is broad and deep, with square, even jaws. To be

in correct balance, the distance from the stop to the tip
of the nose is one half the distance from the stop up over
the crown to the base of the skull. The nose is black,
brown or liver, the darker the better. The color of the
nose harmonizes with the color of the eye rim.

As set forth by our Standard, the Cocker is to have a
scissors bite. Unfortunately poor bites are prevalent in
the breed. The majority of the bite problems are
undershot. An undershot bite is when the lower jaw is
longer than the upper jaw. The lower and upper jaws
grow at different times and therefore not in sequence.
Some of the problems may be attributed to retained
deciduous (baby) teeth that should be pulled. In my
opinion an off bite seldom causes any health problem.

SIZE

The height of Cockers has grown since the 10-inch
Obo type but some of them didn't know when to stop.
Our Standard says the ideal height of the male is 15
inches at the shoulders and 14 inches for females. They
are to be disqualified from showing if they are more than
half an inch over and to be penalized if they are more
than half an inch under. We see pet Cockers ranging in
height from 13 to 17-plus inches. Since the height
limitation was incorporated in 1943 there is no reference
to weight in our Standard. You will have a good idea of

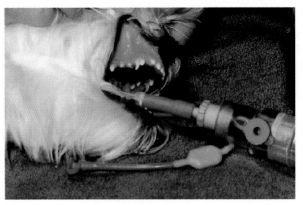

*Retained
deciduous
teeth (puppy
teeth) can be
detrimental
to good bite
formation
and should
be pulled.*

what to expect from your puppy in regards to weight and height if you can see the parents. The 14-inch female usually weighs between 18 and 22 pounds and the 15-inch male weighs approximately 24 to 28 pounds.

ATTITUDE

This may be the most important characteristic of the Cocker Spaniel. The Standard says the Cocker should be "equable in temperament with no

Attitude is probably the most important characteristic of the Cocker Spaniel and potential owners should look for a puppy that is merry.

suggestion of timidity. Above all, he must be free, merry, sound, well-balanced throughout and in action show a keen inclination to work." Many Cockers live up to the Standard but many don't. Heredity and environment play important parts in shaping our Cocker's attitudes. Observing the parents or at least the puppy's dam will give you a good idea of what to expect. It is a good idea to visit with other adult Cockers.

Occasionally a breeder will need to place a puppy because it doesn't have the correct attitude for showing. These puppies are too serious and don't exhibit the merry attitude with a keen inclination to work that our Standard requires. Many of these puppies will be delighted to become companion dogs.

AKC STANDARD FOR THE COCKER SPANIEL

The Board of Directors of the American Kennel Club has approved the following revised Standard for the Cocker Spaniel as submitted by the American Spaniel Club, Inc:

General Appearance

The Cocker Spaniel is the smallest member of the Sporting Group. He has a sturdy, compact body and a cleanly chiseled and refined head, with the overall dog in complete balance and of ideal size. He stands well up at the shoulder on straight forelegs with a topline sloping slightly toward strong, moderately bent, muscular quarters. He is a dog capable of considerable speed, combined with great endurance. Above all, he must be free and merry, sound, well-balanced throughout and in action show a keen inclination to work. A dog well balanced in all parts is more desirable than a dog with strongly contrasting good points and faults.

Size, Proportion, Substance

Size—The ideal height at the withers for an adult dog is 15 inches and for an adult bitch, 14 inches. Height may vary one half inch above or below this ideal. A dog whose height exceeds 15¹/₂ inches or a bitch whose height exceeds 14¹/₂ inches shall be disqualified. An adult dog whose height is less than 13 inches shall be penalized. Height is determined by a line perpendicular to the ground from the top of the shoulder blades, the dog standing naturally with its forelegs and lower hind legs parallel to the line of measurement. *Proportion—*

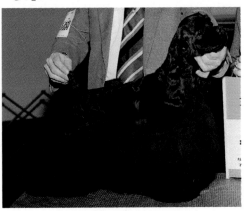

This proud winner has a pleasing expression— intelligent, alert, soft and appealing.

The measurement from the breast bone to back of thigh is slightly longer than the measurement from the highest point of withers to the ground. The body must be of sufficient length to permit a straight and free stride; the dog never appears long and low.

The Cocker Spaniel must have a well-proportioned head that is in balance with the rest of the dog.

Head

To attain a well proportioned head, which must be in balance with the rest of the dog, it embodies the following: *Expression*—The expression is intelligent, alert, soft and appealing. *Eyes*—Eyeballs are round and full and look directly forward. The shape of the eye rims gives a slightly almond shaped appearance; the eye is not weak or goggled. The color of the iris is dark brown and in general the darker the better. *Ears*—Lobular, long, of fine leather, well feathered and placed no higher than a line to the lower part of the eye. *Skull*—Rounded but not exaggerated with no tendency toward flatness; the eyebrows are clearly defined with a pronounced stop. The bony structure beneath the eyes is well chiseled with no prominence in the cheeks. The muzzle is broad and deep, with square, even jaws. To be in correct balance, the distance from the stop to the tip of the nose is one half the distance from the stop up over the crown to the base of the skull. *Nose*—of sufficient size to balance the muzzle and foreface, with well developed nostrils typical of a sporting dog. It is black in color in the blacks, black and tans, and black and whites; in other colors it may be brown, liver or black, the darker the better. The color of the nose harmonizes with the color of the eye rim. *Lips*—The upper lip is full and of sufficient depth to cover the lower jaw. *Teeth*–Teeth strong and sound, not too small and meet in a scissors bite.

Neck, Topline, Body

Neck–The neck is sufficiently long to allow the nose to reach the ground easily, muscular and free from pendulous "throatiness." It rises strongly from the shoulders and arches slightly as it tapers to join the head. *Topline*–sloping slightly toward muscular quarters. *Body*–the chest is deep, its lowest point no higher than the elbows, its front sufficiently wide for adequate heart and lung space, yet not so wide as to interfere with the straightforward movement of the forelegs. Ribs are deep and well sprung. Back is strong and sloping evenly and slightly downward from the shoulders to the set-on of the docked tail. The docked tail is set on and carried on a line with the topline of the back, or slightly higher; never straight up like a Terrier and never so low as to indicate timidity. When the dog is in motion the tail action is merry.

Forequarters

The shoulders are well laid back forming an angle with the upper arm of approximately 90 degrees which permits the dog to move his forelegs in an easy manner with forward reach. Shoulders are clean cut and sloping

without protrusion and so set that the upper points of the withers are at an angle which permits a wide spring of rib. When viewed from the

The Cocker Spaniel's forelegs are parallel, straight, strongly boned and muscular, set well under the body.

Living up to the standard, Ch. Rendition Triple Play is shown here winning the most prestigious show for a Cocker Spaniel, the American Spaniel Club show.

side with the forelegs vertical, the elbow is directly below the highest point of the shoulder blade. Forelegs are parallel, straight, strongly boned and muscular and set close to the body well under the scapulae. The pasterns are short and strong. Dewclaws on forelegs may be removed. Feet compact, large, round and firm with horny pads; they turn neither in nor out.

Hindquarters

Hips are wide and quarters well rounded and muscular. When viewed from behind, the hind legs are parallel when in motion and at rest. The hind legs are strongly boned, and muscled with moderate angulation at the stifle and powerful, clearly defined thighs. The stifle is strong and there is no slippage of it in motion or when standing. The hocks are strong and well let down. Dewclaws on hind legs may be removed.

Coat

On the head, short and fine; on the body, medium length, with enough undercoating to give protection. The ears, chest, abdomen and legs are well feathered, but not so excessively as to hide the Cocker Spaniel's true lines and movement or affect his appearance and function as a moderately coated sporting dog. The texture is most important. The coat is silky, flat or slightly wavy and of a texture which permits easy care. Excessive coat or curly cottony

The parti-colored coat is made up of two or more solid colors, one of which must be white. This is an example of a black and white.

textured coat shall be severely penalized. Use of electric clippers on the back coat is not desirable. Trimming to enhance the dog's true lines should be done to appear as natural as possible.

Color and Markings

Black Variety—Solid color black to include black with tan points. The black should be jet; shadings of brown or liver in the coat are not desirable. A small amount of white on the chest and/or throat is allowed; white in any other location shall disqualify.

Any Solid Color Other than Black (ASCOB)—Any solid color other than black, ranging from lightest cream to darkest red, including brown and brown

The coat on the Cocker's head should be short and fine, and the ears are well-feathered.

with tan points. The color shall be of a uniform shade, but lighter color of the feathering is permissible. A small amount of white on the chest and/or throat is allowed; white in any other location shall disqualify.

Parti-Color Variety—Two or more solid, well broken colors, one of which must be white; black and white, red and white (the red may range from lightest cream to darkest red), brown and white, and roans, to include any such color combination with tan points. It is preferable that the tan markings be located in the same pattern as for the tan points in the Black and ASCOB varieties. Roans are classified as parti-colors and may be of any of the usual roaning patterns. Primary color which is ninety percent (90%) or more shall disqualify.

Tan Points—The color of the tan may be from the lightest cream to the darkest red and is restricted to ten percent (10%) or less of the color of the specimen; tan markings in excess of that amount shall disqualify. In the case of tan points in the Black or ASCOB variety, the markings shall be located as follows:

1) A clear tan spot over each eye;
2) On the sides of the muzzle and on the cheeks;
3) On the underside of the ears;
4) On all feet and/or legs;
5) Under the tail;
6) On the chest, optional; presence or absence shall not be penalized.

Tan markings which are not readily visible or which amount only to traces shall be penalized. Tan on the muzzle which extends upward, over and joins shall also be penalized. The absence of tan markings in the Black or ASCOB variety in any of the specified locations in any otherwise tan-pointed dog shall disqualify.

Gait
The Cocker Spaniel, though the smallest of the

The buff (light tan) Cocker Spaniel is exhibited in the ASCOB variety. The color should be of a uniform shade, but lighter color of the feathering is permissible.

Sporting Dogs, possesses a typical Sporting Dog gait. Prerequisite to good movement is balance between the front and rear assemblies. He drives with strong, powerful rear quarters and is properly constructed in the shoulders and forelegs so that he can reach forward without constriction in a full stride to counterbalance the driving force from the rear. Above all, his gait is coordinated, smooth and effortless. The dog must cover ground with his action; excessive animation should not be mistaken for proper gait.

This is a fine example of a black and tan head with correct tan markings over the eyes and on the cheeks.

Temperament

Equable in temperament with no suggestion of timidity.

Disqualifications

Height—Males over 15^1/$_2$ inches; females over 14 ^{1}/$_2$ inches.

Color and Markings—The aforementioned colors are the only acceptable colors or combination of colors. Any other colors or combination of such to disqualify.

Black Variety—White markings except on chest and throat.

Any Solid Color Other Than Black Variety—White markings except on chest and throat.

Parti-color Variety—Primary color ninety percent (90%) or more.

Tan Points—(1) Tan markings in excess of ten percent (10%); (2) Absence of tan markings in Black or ASCOB Variety in any of the specified locations in an otherwise tan pointed dog.

SELECTING the Right Cocker Spaniel for You

Reputable breeders do not breed indiscriminately. They do not want to add to the overpopulation of dogs looking for homes. Monetary gain is not their primary objective, but good homes for their puppies are of the utmost importance. A reputable breeder performs the necessary testing to ensure the quality of the breeding. As you may be aware, the Cocker Spaniel was overbred for years, and it has taken responsible breeding to undo the damage. Responsible breeding is the future of the breed.

It is recommended that you try to purchase a puppy from an ASC member or one that follows their standards. The American Spaniel Club has set forth guidelines: *The ASC Code of Ethics* and *Guidelines for Breeding and Purchasing Cocker Spaniels*, which ASC members are expected to abide by. You can contact the ASC secretary, Mrs. Margaret Ciezkowski at 846 Old Stephens Creek Road, Marinez, GA, 30907-9227, for a list of members in your area. The American Kennel Club, 5580 Centerview Drive, Raleigh, NC 27606, (919) 233-9767, would be another source for breeders. Other sources are the local Cocker Spaniel club, the local all-breed kennel club or your veterinarian. Ask about any upcoming shows or puppy matches. These are good places to speak with breeders and seek information about the breed.

The American Spaniel Club recommends that all Cocker Spaniel breeding stock be checked for inherited disorders such as cataracts, progressive retinal atrophy (PRA), hip dysplasia (OFA), hypothyroidism and bleeding disorders. Most of these disorders are present in numerous other breeds and their parent clubs make the same recommendations. The eye exam is performed annually by a veterinary ophthalmologist. An OFA (Orthopedic Foundation for Animals) number is granted for those dogs that are over the age of two years and found to be free of hip dysplasia. The very least you should expect is current (within one year) eye exams on the parents of your puppy. This is not a guarantee that your puppy will remain unafflicted, but it should assure you that the breeder is making a conscientous effort. You may be concerned about these problems but nearly every breed, including mixed breeds, has a predisposition to numerous defects.

An advantage of buying from a reputable breeder is that he will be available for guidance as needed. Reputable breeders want the best for their puppies and want happy, satisfied owners. Recently I had the honor of placing a third puppy with a family who purchased their first one from me in 1978. I always look forward to calls from my

Picking a pumpkin is easier than picking a puppy! Seek out a Cocker puppy from a reputable source that abides by the American Spaniel Club's guidelines.

puppy buyers. It is important to me that I can be of help. Many questions arise regarding feeding, training and grooming. New owners enjoy comparing their puppies to the siblings' progress. Sometimes they meet them at puppy kindergarten class.

Later in life, if a problem arises, it can be of help to know if an ancestor or sibling had a similar problem. You should always notify your breeder if an inherited problem appears in your dog, even if he is elderly. A breeder may not know there is a problem in the bloodline if it hasn't occurred in his own dogs.

THE PEDIGREE

A pedigree is a valuable piece of information that tells of the puppy's ancestry. For the pet owner this is far more important than the AKC registration. The AKC registration states that you own a purebred dog but the pedigree also contains more information. You will

Look for a puppy that is alert and active, displaying bright eyes, a wet nose, and a shiny coat.

Each puppy in a litter has its own personality; it is important to spend time with the puppies before making a final decision in order to choose the one that is right for you.

want to inquire about the health credentials of the ancestors. The pedigree will list the titles (championships, obedience, agility, field, and CGC). This is important. A respectable Cocker pedigree should contain a minimum of 40 to 50 percent champions within the first three or four generations. This may not be the case in other breeds but should be expected in Cockers from good breeding. A pedigree with numerous titled ancestors suggests that they were sound of mind and body and trainable.

Many pet owners express concern about the degree of inbreeding in the Cocker Spaniel. Yes, it is true that at one time the Cocker Spaniel was overly bred and inbred. Upon examination of the pedigree you can determine the amount of inbreeding, linebreeding or outcrossing. Inbreeding is what differentiates one breed from another breed. All purebred dogs are inbred initially to create that particular breed. Some linebreeding is necessary to continue various characteristics within the bloodline.

There have been some excellent dogs produced from inbreedings but the breeder must thoroughly know his bloodlines. Inbreeding is the breeding of parent to offspring or brother to sister, and linebreeding is the breeding together of more distantly related dogs. The problem with inbreeding is that all the faults will be doubled along with the good qualities. An outcross has no common ancestor within the first four generations.

Regardless, most of our bloodlines contain some of the same faults and therefore these faults may appear from outcrossings as well as inbreedings. You will want to discuss this with the breeder. The breeding could produce a lovely puppy or it may be a disaster.

REGISTRATION

Currently many breeders are withholding AKC registrations or are giving limited registration. This enables the breeder to curtail indiscriminate breeding of his offspring. A limited registration restricts entry into some dog events and offspring are not eligible for registration. A limited registered Cocker may compete in obedience, tracking, agility and field trials. Upon application and approval, the AKC will issue an ILP (indefinite listing privilege) to purebred dogs without registration. An ILP is similar to the limited registration.

AGE TO GO TO A NEW HOME

Most prospective buyers set out to buy a six week-old puppy and some sources say that seven weeks is a good age to go to a new home. Usually responsible Cocker breeders prefer to keep their puppies until they are a little older. Some authorities say the eight to nine week period is the fear age and not a good time to go to a new home. Conscientious breeders of show dogs need to hold on to show prospects as long as possible because puppies go through all kinds of changes. It is important that the breeder retains the best breeding potential out of the litter so as to continue the quality of the line.

There are some advantages of taking home a puppy at least ten weeks of age but not older than six months. Lack of social experience may be a potential disadvantage of the six-month or older puppy. The older the puppy the easier it is to housebreak because he is eating fewer meals and therefore needs to potty less frequently. The younger the puppy, the more often he has to relieve himself. Another advantage, if you are dealing with a conscientious breeder, is that the puppy should have had more vaccines, which is a considerable savings to you. Also, presumably your puppy has had frequent groomings, which is part of his training.

Experienced breeders thoroughly know the bloodlines of the dogs they breed. All of the puppies in this litter of Cocker Spaniels became champions.

A puppy's socialization training should begin at five to seven weeks of age. A puppy raised in a kennel environment may have a difficult time adjusting to the real world. Kennel dogs may exhibit fear of all new, non-kennel environments. With proper care these dogs can improve but they may always lack confidence.

I frequently receive calls from people who wish to buy an older, housebroken dog. I always caution these owners to be aware that even though the dog is housebroken in one environment that may not be the case in the new home. You should allow time for the dog to adjust to his new environment and this could be a serious problem for the unneutered male. Making allowances for this knowledge, an older puppy or adult dog can be a perfect pet for the older couple. The new owner should plan on attending a training class to gain the dog's respect. There are some advantages to acquiring the older puppy or adult dog since he has probably completed the series of puppy vaccinations and hopefully is through teething.

You may want to give serious consideration before acquiring a middle age or geriatric dog. As a dog reaches his declining years some medical expense may be incurred. If you haven't formed an attachment to the dog you may not want the financial responsibility. Recently I was asked if I would like to have one of my dogs back at the age of 12. I pointed out to the owner that I didn't feel it was fair to cast the dog off at this time in his life. It is sad that this owner never bonded with his dog.

MALE OR FEMALE?

Prospective owners have definite ideas about which sex of dog they want. Some of their ideas are misconstrued. I receive numerous phone calls saying they have to have a female because they don't want a male who will roam. I explain that females are also

It is not a good idea to have two puppies in the same age group because they will bond to each other rather than their human family.

inclined to roam and no dog should be given that opportunity. Others call and say they have to have a male because of a female's heat cycles. Today's responsible breeder requires his offspring to be spayed and neutered, which makes either sex quite acceptable.

I have found my males to be actually more affectionate and attentive than my females. However, due to my arthritis and bad back I am beginning to have a problem

When searching for a Cocker puppy, do as much research as possible and avoid making a hasty decision but don't pass up the ideal puppy either—they are hard to come by.

with the slightly larger male. That three to five pound difference makes a difference to me. My Cockers are normal size with the girls weighing approximately 20 pounds and the boys 24 to 25 pounds. I do know of some female Cockers that weigh over 30 pounds so it is important to know something about the dogs in the pedigree if the weight is a concern for you.

Some intact male dogs of any breed may be inclined to show a macho behavior, which I personally don't like. (However, females may show signs of dominant behavior, too.) Early neutering, at six months of age, will curtail this behavior and certainly lessen the chance of other undesirable male characteristics such as roaming and marking territory.

Usually a female is a little smaller in height and weight. Again spaying will make her a much better pet and increase her lifespan. I have had people say they don't want a male because of mounting behavior. This is not only a bad habit of males (which can be easily curtailed) but some females are also inclined to mount other dogs and humans. It can be embarrassing but dogs will be dogs. Nevertheless you will want to discourage this behavior at its onset. I have found some of my little girls to be more independent than the boys.

A Puppy is Not Just for Christmas

Some people think it's a great idea to give the children a puppy for Christmas. Actually this is a poor idea. Christmas is a wonderful time of year, full of holiday excitement and all kinds of comings and goings, but it can be really nerve racking for the puppy. Your puppy is joining you as a member of the family for the next 12 to 15 years. It is critical that you give him the attention he deserves and get off to a proper beginning. Wouldn't it be better to wait until after the holiday rush?

Visiting the Breeder

When going to look at puppies there are several things you should check. Are the puppies clean and trimmed? Do they appear healthy? Where are they kept? As pointed out, puppies need a social environment. Many weaned moms look rather sad, especially if they have raised a large litter. You should be able to gauge the dam's temperament. Is she friendly and responsive to you and her owners? Is the seller able to provide you with the necessary health credentials, pedigree and registration? Many breeders require the new owner to sign a contract pertaining to the puppy's welfare. You

The entire family should be a part of the puppy picking process.

should feel free to ask questions regarding the ancestors, health, training, grooming, and last but not least the temperament.

Nine-month-old Ch. Sandor's Oreo Delight, UDTX, owned by the author.

More Than One

Frequently folks come for a puppy and then ask about acquiring a littermate or a second puppy elsewhere. I discourage this from the beginning. It is not a good idea to have two puppies in the same age group because in all probability they will be quick to bond to each other and not to the human family. It is important that each new puppy has the opportunity to go through the bonding individually. Another consideration is when there are two dogs around the same age, eventually they may leave you within the same time span. I usually advise people to wait until their dog is around three years of age before acquiring a second dog. This seems to work out quite well. Some sources recommend getting a dog of the opposite sex, thinking they will adjust better. Personally I am not sure how significant this is if both dogs are spayed and neutered. When the second dog comes home it is necessary to think of your first dog. You shouldn't neglect him or subject him to unending puppy exuberance. The dogs need to become accustomed to each other gradually. When the puppy gets a little overbearing, it is time for him to take "time out" in his crate.

Temperament Testing

Very few puppy buyers have the opportunity or the knowledge to temperament test an entire litter. Frequently the experienced breeder is going to be the best judge of which puppy will fit into a particular environment. For instance, the soft, shy puppy may do better in a family without children. The more outgoing puppy has a better chance of adjusting to children than his more reserved littermate.

GROWTH OF PUPPY

Puppies grow rapidly. During the growth period you should watch your puppy's weight. Extra fat can be harmful to the growing joints. Your puppy will probably reach at least half of his adult size by five months of age and will reach full height before a year of age, probably around nine months. At that time his body will continue to fill out and mature. Around this time, depending on when he reaches puberty, his puppy coat will shed out and his adult coat will come in. During this time the coat will take extra care to keep from matting severely. Many Cockers' adult coats are never as plush as their puppy coats and consequently are not successful in the show ring.

Before selecting a puppy, observe good examples of the breed. This tri-color has gorgeous markings and a beautiful head.

Be prepared when selecting a puppy. Do as much research as possible and don't make a hasty decision but don't pass up the ideal puppy. Sometimes they are hard to find. Cocker registrations are down as we strive for better quality.

At five and a half months of age this Cocker pup is already preparing for a career in agility.

CHARACTERISTICS of the Cocker Spaniel

I grew up with a Cocker Spaniel and to this day I would not consider owning another breed. I seriously doubt if any other breed could fill my Cocker's footprints or its place in my heart. Obviously many others feel as I do or the breed would not have retained its popularity for over half a century. At least weekly I run into people who claim their Cocker is the best dog they ever owned.

The Cocker Spaniel is the smallest member of the Sporting Group but it will never go unnoticed. A few of the Sporting dogs are more hunting and retrieving oriented but none is a better companion dog. The Cocker's keen nose is always at work in the field or around the house. Owners talk about their Cockers finding toys that have been misplaced for weeks.

The Cocker's small size makes it a perfect house or apartment dog. As a matter of fact it should not be left outside since it may get into mischief. Since the Cocker is very people oriented, it much prefers being around its human family. A Cocker thrives on companionship and shouldn't be denied it. Frequently it is at its owner's heels, following from room to room. There is no doubt about it—the lovable Cocker is a wonderful family dog.

Cocker Spaniels are happiest around their owners and people they know. Ashley and Scarlett are best friends.

CHILDREN

Cockers can do very well around children if they are raised with them. Toddlers and adult dogs of any breed can present a problem if they have not had adequate exposure as puppies. Many dogs will be a little nervous with all the fast moves children make. I have a concern of placing a young puppy in a family with a toddler since I am worried the child may

Although most Cockers will merrily share a kiss with a toddler friend, adults should carefully supervise interaction for the child's safety.

Besides its classic beauty, the Cocker Spaniel has many characteristics that make it one of the most popular dogs today.

treat the small puppy as a stuffed animal and carry him around all day. This recently happened with my two-year-old grandson. At first he was very interested and conscientious, and

Cocker Spaniels are well mannered dogs that make wonderful house pets. Their small size makes them ideal for apartment living.

then, after a day or two, he lost interest and wasn't as gentle. Fortunately, my puppy was only visiting for socializing purposes. In this case the toddler could not cope with the young puppy. This type of environment needs strict parental supervision. In all probability it would be better to wait until the youngster is a bit older. However, my grandson arrived after his parents' dog (who was two at the time) and now the two of them truly enjoy playing together. They are the best of friends!

Children should be taught good manners towards dogs, which includes no teasing, roughhousing or screaming. It takes work but the youngster needs to learn to be as calm as humanly possible for his age around dogs. A child should never be left unsupervised with a dog and should never put his face in the dog's face. All children should learn respect not only for their family dog but for strange dogs as well. Precaution is better than a mishap that could have been prevented.

PERSONALITY

Even though Cockers are very merry little dogs, some are happiest around their owners and people they know. It is amazing how long their memory is when it comes to remembering people even though they see them infrequently. A few Cockers are shy around strangers, meaning they have to be the one to approach the stranger. There are those who never do take that first step and hover around their owners. This issue shouldn't be forced.

The Cocker Spaniel should not be left outside unsupervised since he may get into mischief.

There was a time when too many Cockers were outwardly aggressive but fortunately this is becoming history. In my opinion the temperaments have greatly improved. We can attribute this to more selective breeding and the concentrated effort on the owner's part of attending puppy kindergarten and obedience classes. Today we see many bubbly Cockers—probably the ideal temperament—although some folks don't appreciate their exuberance.

EAGER TO PLEASE

A wonderful characteristic of the breed is its eagerness to please. This is important to Cockers. Some dogs will be utterly crushed if they feel they aren't living up to your expectations. I remember training one of my first utility dogs. Utility work is very difficult and the dog makes numerous mistakes while learning. Every time I needed to correct Duchess (I might add they were mild corrections) I swear she cried and that hurt me. As you might suspect she had a very soft personality. Eventually she learned that corrections were a part of daily life and I really did love her. In retrospect I see this type of training made her into a superior dog. There was a very strong bond between us that existed throughout her life.

Cockers are intelligent and quick to learn. However, they can be a little stubborn when they need to unlearn something that has been learned incorrectly. It takes patience and repetition, but the end result is worth the effort. My pet owners are always astonished at their Cocker's intelligence.

COCKERS CAN DO IT ALL

The majority of our Cockers are devoted companion dogs. A smaller percentage of them start out with show careers in conformation and obedience, which usually prove to be quite successful, before retiring to the easy life. A much smaller group is trained for hunting by a few dedicated breeders and owners. Through their efforts, Cockers are preserving the inherent hunting instinct of their ancestors from centuries ago. Even after retirement I feel Cockers would rather stay active then sleep all day.

The Cocker was originally bred as a hunting dog and then became a show dog and a companion dog. The nose never stops working. Would you believe I know of at least one Cocker Spaniel that worked airports sniffing for drugs? I know the majority of my dogs have very keen noses, which have earned us numerous tracking titles. We have out-tracked some good tracking breeds. Cockers have physical and mental stamina although in some cases the mental stamina needs to be developed. In general, Cockers are very energetic and this energy needs to be channeled in the right direction.

A fairly new sport is agility. Cockers love it and do quite well flying over the course. I have found agility to relieve stress for those dogs that are in other types of competition and it is also a confidence builder. It is fun and like any dog activity, it takes team work.

Who is the Ideal Owner?

Cockers need an environment with love and companionship. With parental supervision they do very well in a family with children. I have placed many Cockers with senior citizens who exist for their dogs. The majority of our Cockers are very active throughout their lives until their own senior citizen days. Therefore it is nice to place the younger dog with a family who can give it attention and a chance to play. Play time is important for any dog.

Properly socialized Cocker Spaniels do well in multi-dog households.

Some prospective owners voice concern about acquiring a puppy and fitting it into an already hectic schedule. It is true that when possible it would be a good idea to arrange getting the new pup/dog during vacation time being spent at home or at the beginning of a long weekend. It is not advisable to take the new puppy home, only to have to board it in a couple of weeks because you are going on vacation. An exception would be if the puppy could be boarded at the breeder's. Puppies go through many periods of adjustments, not only physical growth periods but also mental growth periods. It would be a good idea to discuss this with your breeder. You wouldn't want to traumatize him at such an early age.

Probably a major concern is for the new pet owner to work out schedules to care for the young puppy while trying to work a full-time job. There is no question about it—it would be better if someone could be home during the day to exercise and feed the puppy (if he is of age to need to eat during the day). Over the years I have sold numerous puppies to people who work full-time jobs and the puppies did nicely. I am gone for long hours during the day, which is hard on my dogs, but we all survive. I make up for it by spending quality time with them before and after work. When they are very young I try to find a neighbor to let them out during the day but if I can't, they do okay. It just takes a little longer to crate train them, but that is unavoidable in the young puppy left for long periods of time.

Some dogs, not just Cockers, can be a wee bit stubborn and therefore need a "strong hand." I am not referring to physical correction but to constructive education with positive reinforcement. It is important that the owner be consistent in giving commands so the dog will not be confused by mixed signals. This involves the entire family. In my opinion some of the nicest people own the worst behaved dogs, which is the result of being "too kind." The owner is afraid to correct his dog and therefore the dog takes advantage of the situation. It is far kinder to train the dog to be a good citizen.

The new Cocker owner must be prepared to be the Alpha. This is most important. Cockers are very intelligent and because of this there is the occasional dog that will take advantage of his owner. By all means not all dogs are so inclined. It is amazing how many owners are intimidated by their puppies. These owners are usually lacking in dog experience.

The Cocker owner must be prepared to not only train his dog and give it veterinary care as needed but he needs to see to the grooming of his dog as well. This can be done at home or professionally. Cockers are labeled a high-maintenance dog primarily because of the required grooming. This does not have to be a horrendous task if the coat is kept up. I find I can keep my long-coated Cockers in satisfactory shape by a thorough combing every four to six days. Of course, more often is better.

THE COCKER SPANIEL TODAY

Agility is a fairly new sport. Cockers love it and do quite well flying over the course.

All Cocker breeders desire their dogs to be good ambassadors of the breed. It is an old breed that has withstood the test of time. The Cocker has survived because of its

lovable nature, intelligence, trainability, compact size and, last but not least, its beauty. It is each Cocker owner's responsibility to prepare his dog to be such an ambassador. Cocker owners are proud of their dogs.

Cockers make ideal therapy dogs. After being certified as a pet therapy dog and passing the Canine Good Citizen test they are eligible to visit nursing homes, hospitals, etc. Their visits are greatly enjoyed and they spread good will.

Cockers are intelligent and quick to learn. Here Barney shows off his new trick.

Cocker Spaniels excel in the show ring but this isn't necessarily the life for most of them. Conformation showing isn't easy and you should respect the dog that has achieved championship status. It wasn't an easy road to travel. Cockers do enjoy obedience training and showing, which is available to all our dogs. Agility is the newest sport and is lots of fun for both the dog and owner. Tracking is great exercise for that same team, but certainly isn't for everyone (although it is my favorite dog sport). During the last decade or two breeders have been trying to cultivate an interest in hunting, which had nearly become extinct for the modern Cocker.

Even though the Cocker is quite capable of performing in all these sports and is easily trained, the majority of our Cockers are well deserving companion dogs. Today the Cocker Spaniel is better than ever before!

Cockers do very well with children, especially if they are raised together. With only one month difference in age, these two toddlers will grow up together.

FEEDING Your Cocker Spaniel

Cocker Spaniels do best if they are fed the same diet daily. Some Cockers have sensitive digestive tracts and the slightest change in food results in diarrhea.

Most breeders send some of the puppy's food with him so he doesn't have to change his diet. If the puppy is being fed a premium growth type diet, you may want to continue this. If you feel it is necessary to change to a different brand of food you will need to wean him over a period of about a week. This involves decreasing the customary food and adding the new food in small allotments. This concept is extremely important to avoid a GI upset. You may want to check with a veterinarian for his recommendation on which diet to feed. Do not give your puppy milk. Milk can cause diarrhea in puppies over the age of six weeks. After that time they no longer have the enzymes necessary to digest it.

Learning good feeding manners should begin during puppyhood. Cory is showing good manners by waiting patiently for his food.

I am a firm believer in allowing the puppy to eat in his crate, allowing approximately 15 minutes to finish his food. When this procedure is followed, puppies learn to be good eaters. Puppies are, by nature, little busy bodies and therefore when allowed to eat outside the crate they tend to eat a few bites and then run around, only to return to eat another bite and so it goes. The crate prevents distractions and the puppy doesn't feel his food is threatened by children or other pets. If the puppy doesn't finish his food within his time allowance, then you should discard it and shouldn't feed him treats or his dinner until his next scheduled time.

Learning good feeding manners should begin during

puppyhood. Teach him that it is okay for you to take away his food but give it back right away. Hand feed him a piece of kibble or a treat and teach him not to grab. As he matures, ask him to sit and wait patiently for his food and reward him with praise and of course his food bowl. I like to feed puppies in either crock bowls or stainless steel pans. Plastic bowls are too tempting to teething puppies.

Schedule: at eight weeks of age Cocker puppies can do quite well on three meals a day (i.e., 7 AM, noon, and 6 PM), feeding $1/2$ cup of dry kibble (puppy diet) per feeding. At 16 weeks of age many puppies can graduate to two feedings of about 1 cup per meal. Around eight months of age most Cocker puppies can be fed once a day if that is your desire. Some pet owners prefer to continue two feedings per day even for their adults. Your puppy's feeding habits will determine when and how much to feed. When he begins to lose his appetite is an indication to decrease his feedings and/or amount.

The dinner bell is ringing and this hungry Cocker comes running with dish in mouth.

When my puppies in the eight to 12 month age group lose interest in the puppy diet, I know it is time to wean them to adult food.

THE ADULT

My adult Cockers do very well eating once a day, about 1 to 2 cups of a high-quality maintenance food. Most dogs can do nicely on one meal a day but there are some who will vomit a bile-like fluid in between meals. These dogs may do better on two meals a day. I adjust the quantity fed by feeling the fat over the dog's ribs and hip bones. You should be able to feel the ribs. If you have difficulty in feeling the ribs, your dog is overweight; if you can't feel the ribs, he is obese.

A sign of a healthy dog is one that is hungry all the time. This Cocker eagerly awaits his next meal.

I do not believe in free feeding if for no other reason then that it makes housebreaking more difficult. It is so much easier to housebreak a dog that eats on a regular schedule. Free feeding encourages poor eating habits and may contribute to obesity since most Cockers like to eat. A sign of a healthy dog is one that acts hungry all the time therefore it is better for your dog to become accustomed to a schedule. Whatever you do, don't encourage him to beg at the table. In the past I have used this time to practice the long down with some of my Cockers. They were placed in the long down away from the table and seldom interfered with our meals. Once in a while I would have to leave the table to reinforce the command, but it didn't take long for them to catch on.

THE SENIOR CITIZEN

These dogs will benefit from a diet lower in protein and phosphorus and possibly containing more fiber.

Most dog food manufacturers make several kinds of diets for the different life stages so this should be easy to find. The senior years shouldn't be obese years but in my opinion your dog will do better carrying some reserve weight. After a certain time in his life he will stop gaining and needs the reserve to fall back on when he begins the actual decline. Speak to your veterinarian about his weight and the best diet for him.

In the past I have owned a couple of older Cockers that showed signs of kidney problems although their laboratory work didn't confirm this. Occasionally laboratory tests may be a little behind the actual symptoms. After speaking with my veterinarian we decided they might benefit from a prescription kidney diet and they did quite well, living longer than I expected. Their symptoms were PD/PU, which means drinking a lot of water and consequently urinating frequently, and were very pronounced before the change of diet; the symptoms decreased after the change in diet.

Feeling the fat over the rib spring is a good way to measure a dog's weight. You should be able to feel the ribs.

OBESITY

There is no excuse for letting a Cocker become obese and unfortunately too many of them are. This is the owner's fault. As previously mentioned, the sign of a healthy dog is one that is always hungry but that does not require you to give in to him. I am always amazed when a few (fortunately very few) of my owners say "Beau doesn't want to eat his food," so they doctor his food up with goodies. I speak from

Proper nutrition is essential for the good health of your Cocker Spaniel.

experience when I say I'm not interested in vegetables but fast foods when I am overweight. I look for something more exotic than the basics. It is the same for our dogs. Don't give in. Your veterinarian can suggest a good diet, higher in fiber and lower in calories. If your dog expects treats, then measure out his daily ration of food and hand out the treats from that allowance. He probably won't be too interested if he is overweight (he'll be looking for the "gourmet" type) but as he begins to lose weight his appetite will increase and regular food will seem more appealing. You can add canned carrots or green beans to his meals.

Obesity is a major contributor to diseases such as those of the heart, circulatory system, liver, and pancreas as well as diabetes. It certainly lessens the chance of successful anesthetic and surgical procedures. The obese dog may have trouble breathing and suffer heat intolerance. An overweight Cocker may be more at risk for spinal and joint problems such as torn ligaments and arthritis. You will prolong your Cocker's life by keeping him within normal weight

Carrots are good fillers for those watching their weight or in this case for a four-month-old teething pup.

You should feed a good commercial diet or a recipe (for special dietary cases) that is veterinary approved.

limits. If you are feeding your Cocker a minimum amount of a low calorie food and he is still overweight it may be a good idea to consult your veterinarian about hypothyroid testing. Lack of exercise and low thyroid are major contributors to obesity.

SUPPLEMENTS

If you are feeding a well-balanced premium food, supplements are not necessary and may even be harmful. Vitamins and other supplements can unbalance the balanced diet. Feeding two or more different types of diets can also unbalance the balanced diet. Excessive nutrition can stunt growth or can over-stimulate growth leading to bone and joint problems. It can also predispose or further the progression of diseases such as those of the kidney, heart, vascular system, bladder and skin. More is not necessarily better.

WATER

I am sure it goes without saying that fresh clean water should be available all the time. Water is the most important of all nutrients. The only exception to the availability of water would be withholding it during the night for the young puppy, which might aid the puppy in keeping his crate dry during the night. All my crated dogs have stainless steel water pails hanging in their crates. Otherwise they would "tank up" on it when they have access, which could lead to vomiting. The hanging water pail doesn't tip over and also keeps the ears dry, which is another plus. Even after the dog has graduated from the crate the water pail is still nice for these reasons.

COMMERCIAL PET FOODS

Heaven only knows how dogs survived years ago when they existed on such a concoction of who knows what. I know approximately 20 to 25 years ago I was still feeding a cereal mixture to my puppies. In this country we are fortunate to have some very good commercial diets. I certainly don't recommend you try to make your own diet unless you are given a veterinary approved recipe.

Be careful not to overfeed your Cocker Spaniel as the breed is prone to obesity. Here Bogie is getting his weekly "weigh in."

There are four different types of commercial pet foods:

1. generic
2. private label
3. popular brands (those marketed in grocery and feed stores)
4. premium brands (those marketed in pet stores and veterinary clinics)

A snood (or in this case a cut off sock) keeps the ears clean while eating.

My recommendation is to feed a premium brand that is a fixed formula. A fixed formula is one that always has the same ingredients and in the same amounts. I have fed variable formula foods in the past and my Cockers have suffered digestive upsets each time I opened a new bag of food. The ingredients in variable formula diets vary depending on the cost of the ingredients at the time of manufacture. The diet is inconsistent. Usually the popular pet foods are variable formula diets.

Commercial foods come in three forms: dry, semi-moist and canned. The dry foods help prevent plaque formation on the teeth, which aids in healthier gums and teeth. In many cases this lessens the frequency of periodic dental treatments. A premium dry food also produces a firmer stool and decreases stool frequency (easier clean up).

Canned food is high in water content and sodium nitrate, acting like a diuretic in some dogs. It is highly palatable but does nothing to help your dog's teeth and it is costly compared to dry food. It may deter housebreaking because of the larger stool volume.

Semi-moist foods are very convenient, produce a large stool volume, do nothing to help the teeth and again are expensive compared to dry food. Semi-moist foods are very palatable because they are rich in sugar.

They do have a long shelf life due to the high preservative content. Some foods, including the semi-moist, canned and some of the dry diets have a lot of artificial coloring, which may be difficult to clean up after an accident.

Feeding your Cocker puppy dry food helps prevent plaque formation on the teeth, which aids in healthier gums and teeth.

HYPOALLERGENIC DIETS

Some authorities claim the Cocker Spaniel is the number one breed for food allergies. Many owners and breeders are quick to jump on the "bandwagon" with the new lamb diets. My best advice to you is to refrain from changing diets. Dogs develop an allergy through exposure to the protein in the diet. You shouldn't expose your Cocker prematurely to different proteins because if he develops an allergy you may have a difficult time finding a protein to which he hasn't been exposed. Symptoms of food allergy are skin and ear problems. Unfortunately I have a dog diagnosed with food allergy and her only symptom is swelling of one ear. Allergies are not to be taken lightly and if you suspect you have a problem you need to discuss it with your veterinarian or the dermatologist. The protein source in the hypoallergenic diets may be lamb, venison, duck or fish. However, you shouldn't select a diet without checking the other ingredients. It is possible there may be other potential allergens in the diet.

Feeding your Cocker Spaniel puppy in the crate prevents distractions, and the puppy doesn't feel his food is threatened by children and other pets.

HOUSEBREAKING Your Puppy

D id you ever child-proof your house? It is now time to puppy-proof! Puppies are little explorers and capable of all kinds of mischief. It is amazing what they will find, let alone destroy. Normal behavior for all puppies is to chew and teethe on anything within reach, whether it be furniture, carpet, toys, books, etc. Owners are the ones accountable for their misdeeds because at this age they don't know right from wrong. The crate is the safest environment for all unsupervised puppies. It is truly unfortunate that so many dogs end up in shelters because of their destructive behavior. They never had the proper upbringing.

Do not make the mistake of giving your puppy old shoes or other personal articles to chew. He cannot distinguish between the acceptable old shoe and the brand new one. Try to encourage him to chew on Nylabones® or Gumabones®. I do not believe in rawhides because they can cause GI upset and have occasionally resulted in intestinal blockage. However, a new product, Roar-Hide™ by Nylabone®, is very hard and safe for your Cocker Spaniel. My dogs enjoy squeaky toys but some of them are not happy until they "kill" the squeaky. Tara is partial to a particular toy that she has had for two years but she will quickly destroy any other toy. When giving these types of toys, you need to supervise and take them away when the playing turns to chewing.

Back to puppy-proofing. Puppies love to teethe on electrical cords. One of the puppies I sold did just that (at six months of age) and electrocuted himself. The owner found him unconscious but fortunately she was able to resuscitate him and he survived after receiving medical treatment. If he had been under her direct supervision this wouldn't have happened.

Another mischief puppies enjoy is ingesting foreign objects. This is a real problem when there are young children with toys. I have known puppies to raid the dog food bin or garbage and bloat from overeating. They have been known to drink out of toilets that contained toxic cleaning chemicals. For those of you who have swimming pools or creeks, beware—your puppy may not be able to save himself.

CRATE TRAINING

Crates are a must. I have sold many puppies and always recommend they use a crate but a few owners have declined. Within a day or two I receive a call asking if they can borrow one and I am greatly relieved. A crate will definitely help with house training and it provides a safe environment for your puppy. However, your dog should never wear a collar while crated because there is always a chance it could catch on something. The exception to this could be the fiberglass crate with nothing in it such

Metal crates such as this one allow more air and give the residents a better view of their surroundings.

as a water pail or grate. When using a metal crate there is the occasional puppy that will work the top loose. Susie's middle name is "Houdini" since she always manages to work the top loose and consequently gets her head stuck. To prevent this I secure it with snaps.

I prefer the metal crates but the fiberglass crates are less expensive. Metal crates allow more air and give the resident a better view of his surroundings. The best size for the fiberglass crate is 27"L x 20"W x 19"H although you may prefer the larger size 32"L x 22"W x 23"H if you own a male. I use two different sizes of metal crates 24"L x 18"W x 21"H and 30"L x 18"W x 21"H depending on whether it is a female or a male. When using the crate for house training purposes, the puppy will learn quicker in a smaller crate since a puppy doesn't like to soil his living area. If the crate is too large it is possible for him to soil one area and stay clean at the other end.

Most puppies readily accept the crate and consider it to be their personal "house." Frequently puppies and adults will seek solitude on their own by taking "time out" in the crate. There are some basic rules for crate training. The first rule is to always exercise your puppy IMMEDIATELY when removing him from the crate. (You may need to refrain from speaking to the very young puppy because he may be so excited that he may inadvertently piddle.) Also, you should always exercise him before putting him in the crate. It surely wouldn't be fair to confine him when he

Many common houseplants are poisonous to dogs. When puppy-proofing your house make sure to move plants out of the puppy's reach.

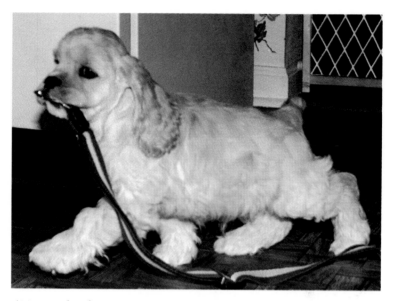

At ten weeks of age this well-trained Cocker pup is letting his owner know that he needs to go outside—the leash is a dead giveaway.

needs to potty. I have found puppies learn to hold it for longer periods of time while crated. When they have freedom, young puppies tend to piddle every 15 to 20 minutes.

It is a good idea to give your dog a few safe toys but in my opinion you shouldn't give him any bedding. If the puppy has an accident, the bedding will absorb it and he still stays clean, which doesn't encourage good crate training. Puppies and some older dogs enjoy chewing on any bedding left in their crates.

House training can begin at seven or eight weeks of age. This should go smoothly for a healthy puppy free of worms and who eats a premium puppy diet without variations. Bad habits are hard to break and training a puppy to use newspaper is one such habit. Puppies that are newspaper trained prefer it to going outside.

The younger the puppy, the more frequently he needs to go out. Plan on exercising him first thing in the morning and last thing in the evening and after every meal. When he is free in the house you ideally should

Do not make the mistake of giving your puppy an old shoe to chew on. This habit will be hard to break and may lead your dog to believe that all shoes are fair game—new or old.

take him out every 30 minutes up to the age of about three months. His trips outside will decrease as he grows up.

ELIMINATE ON COMMAND

Yes, this is possible and simplifies life. Always take your puppy/dog out on leash to relieve himself. If he is very young, you may need to carry him to the designated area. It is helpful to return to the same area where he has pottied before and use the command "go potty" or "hurry up." All young puppies are willing to cooperate and do not object to the leash.

Problems arise when you allow your dog freedom (off leash) to investigate the yard and choose his own area. When this occurs there is the possibility he will refuse to relieve himself while on leash. There will be occasions when you need him to exercise in areas away from home (such as a rest area on a trip, before entering the veterinarian's office, etc.) and it will not be safe to let him go off leash. I have known more than one dog that has been let out in the yard only to run around and then come back in the house to relieve himself. It is much simpler and less time consuming, especially in the rain, if your dog is trained to relieve himself on leash command.

However, if your dog doesn't cooperate when you take him out he must be returned to his crate for another walk outside about 30 to 35 minutes later.

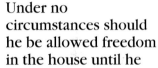

Frequently puppies as well as adult dogs will seek solace in the crate. Iris is spending time teething on her Nylabone®. Note the water pail and sanitary floor.

Under no circumstances should he be allowed freedom in the house until he has done his business. In the house, your puppy will usually circle looking for a place to go. When you see this behavior, pick him up and rush him outside.

It may be more difficult to teach the older dog the eliminate on command concept than the on-leash concept. An older dog has the ability to hold it longer, which complicates the issue. Teach your puppy while he is young. There is much to gain. Also remember to exercise your puppy before you take him to the groomer, veterinarian, etc. Many dogs tend to get nervous and are inclined to have accidents easily.

Scolding

It is your job to prevent accidents by keeping your puppy on schedule and anticipating his needs. You cannot expect very young puppies to have much control but as they mature so do their potty habits. While I am at work my four-month-old puppies still piddle during the day, but when I am home during the day they stay clean. In my opinion, scolding does nothing to encourage house training and may make it worse by making the puppy submissive.

Submissive Urination

This occurs in some Cocker Spaniels as well as many other breeds. The best way to handle it is to try to ignore your dog if he hasn't had a chance to piddle recently. For instance, if you have been gone all day, obviously your dog is going to be very excited to see you. After arriving home, immediately take him out to exercise. Then gauge the amount of affection you bestow on him. When your dog shows a tendency towards submissive urination you will only encourage this problem if you shower him with affection. Also, you will encourage the same reaction if you scold him each time he piddles. It is best to ignore the situation, prepare accordingly and the habit will more than likely get better. I always tell people to take their dogs out to exercise before company arrives. It helps prevent accidents.

Clean Ups

Always blot up the piddle with paper towels and then use a solution of white vinegar and water or one of the products available from your veterinarian or pet shop. Do not pick up stool in front of your puppy. I feel this could encourage coprophagia (stool eating).

Fenced-In Yard

Do not depend on your fenced-in yard as a means of

house training your puppy. Leaving the puppy out for long periods of time allows him to piddle frequently, which does nothing for improving his holding capacity. Cockers do not do well left outside and are inclined to learn quickly to go under or over fences. A plus for the fenced-in yard is that in most circumstances it will keep stray dogs out, which means they won't exercise in your yard and leave intestinal parasites. Under no circumstances should you trust the fence to keep male dogs away from your girl if she should be in heat.

BEING A GOOD NEIGHBOR

The good neighbor shows consideration and doesn't allow his dog to relieve himself in his neighbors' yards or allow him to run loose. In

Don't allow your Cocker Spaniel to run loose. In most states being off leash is against the law.

most states being off leash is against the law. If you have a problem with your neighborhood children teasing your dog, try to explain calmly to their families why this disturbs your dog.

I own several dogs and when one barks the others join the chorus. Because I get up before the roosters I close the windows in my house (while I am exercising the dogs) so the barking doesn't carry through the neighborhood. If you only own one or two dogs this shouldn't be a problem for you. However, if you live in close surroundings and your Cocker is inclined to bark you should try to discourage it and possibly leave the radio or TV on for his entertainment during the day. One habit I truly dislike is the dog that arrives at our clinic barking his head off while the owner makes no attempt at correcting him.

EQUIPMENT

If you have just acquired a new puppy/dog you need to consider purchasing a pooper scooper. You will decrease the incidence of intestinal parasites by cleaning up your yard daily with a pooper scooper. Don't forget to carry baggies with you for pick up when away from home.

Also, for training your puppy, you will need a collar and a 6-foot leather leash. Do not get a chain lead as it will hurt your hands when you are trying to make leash corrections. In most instances retractable leashes interfere with successful training, especially for controlled heeling. However, they are useful in some advanced training exercises. For young puppies, I like the snap-buckle nylon-web collars, which are easier to put on than the old fashioned buckle collars. Later, for more serious training, you will need a regular choke chain training collar. My girls usually wear a 14- or a 16-inch collar and the boys wear a 16-inch. In a properly fitted collar you only want about 2 inches left over. If you find it tight, remember to put it on over one ear at a time. Most training classes will help fit your dog or include the collar and leash in the cost of the class. If you intend to give conformation class a try, you need to purchase a $^3/_8$ inch nylon-web show lead. Point of interest, please remember if a dog decides to balk, it can slip the show lead and the buckle collar but not the choke collar. For that reason I only use the choke collar. You should never leave a choke collar on an unattended dog because it can get caught.

EXERCISE

Cocker Spaniels do need daily exercise but not nearly as much as the larger breeds. They will benefit from a daily walk. However, I do not recommend jogging on hard pavement as it is stressful to the joints. If your time is limited, playing ball (letting him chase the ball several times a day) may suffice. Your dog's weight, attitude and physical health will be your guide to his exercise requirements. Regular exercise is needed not only to keep him in proper weight, but to

Many Cockers love the water. These two are getting their sea legs after a swim.

maintain good heart and lung function and good muscle tone.

Many Cockers love to swim although mine were virtually afraid of the water. I taught them to swim by going in the water, keeping them on a nylon collar and leash, and leading them in to where they couldn't touch bottom. Initially they panic and bring the front feet and head out of the water, treading with their hind feet. A dog needs to keep his head at the water line to swim properly. In the beginning it is helpful to have him carry a bumper or stick, which will keep his head down. Swimming is another form of exercise, along with playing. It is a great way of exercising dogs that have joint problems since there is no stress on the joints. You need to take precautions if you have a swimming pool since there is the possibility that he may fall in and not be able to get out. It would be a good idea to place a large marker at the steps and train him to find it.

Cockers are playful by nature. Unfortunately there are a few who are not interested in toys but those that do thrive on retrieving them and thereby gain your attention. Many will play by themselves, dropping the ball off the sofa and jumping down to get it. Play time is important and is another way of communicating with your dog. Don't neglect it.

TRAINING Your Cocker Spaniel

ll puppies should attend a puppy kindergarten class that will teach some beginning obedience training. In class, your dog will be meeting strangers and learning to interact with members of his own species. After PKT, it is wise to attend at least one basic obedience class, and if you like it, then class never has to end. Cockers can do quite well in the all obedience classes and at obedience trials. If you are interested and your puppy shows potential, you may want to give conformation classes and showing a try. Dog people are wonderful and it is nice to share experiences with each other.

CONFORMATION

You can practice alone but for sure you will need guidance. The goal is to get your dog to strut his stuff by gaiting properly with a show-off attitude. Some start off with this attitude and others acquire attitude through experience.

It is important to know how to show your dog to its best advantage. This is how you would stack your Cocker Spaniel for a judge to view and examine.

A Cocker is supposed to hold his head high on a somewhat loose lead and move in a straight line, preferably a little in front of the handler. He is gaited on your left side and the usual show ring

In the ring, the Cocker Spaniel handler would hold up the ears to show off the length of the neck to the judge.

patterns are an "L" or a triangle. The judge wants to observe your dog from the side (checking his topline, which is to be slightly sloping from shoulder to croup), from the front (to see if he is moving straight and that neither foot or elbow is turning in or out), and from the rear (checking to see if he is moving straight not too wide or narrow and making sure his hocks and/or feet are not turning in or out). His tail should be up and wagging. Your dog needs to learn to gait by himself, in front of and behind other dogs. This can be a challenge if your dog likes to be in front or if your dog is too interested in the dog behind him.

In the show ring the dogs always move counter

clockwise to the left. My dogs learn to anticipate and cut the corners so I usually practice going to the right, sometimes with the dogs on my left and sometimes on my right. It helps. The most important part of training and showing is to make it fun for your dog so he keeps up his attitude and doesn't get bored. I have found some preliminary obedience training, not enforcing the sit at heel or keeping the dog at heel position, gives my dogs confidence and encourages them to behave better.

The judge will examine your dog on a table and check out his bone structure, muscle tone, condition, bite and the texture of his coat, etc. Dogs need to be trained to stand still in "stack" position and let strangers go over them. You will learn about this in conformation class.

OBEDIENCE

Every dog should learn some basic commands such as to sit/stay, down/stay, stand/stay, heel and come. The most important command a dog can learn is to come.

Recall or Come

Teach this exercise by putting your dog on leash and calling him, "Beau, come." You may need to get down to his level since dogs worry about those who tower over them. If he doesn't come, then reel him in on the leash. Don't reach for him but let him touch you first. If you grab for him, he may not be willing to come the next time. Always praise him when he responds and giving a treat would be in order. **Never correct your dog when he comes to you—even if he has been naughty.** If you punish him, he probably won't be willing to come in the future.

Sit/Stay

Your dog needs to learn to sit on command and there are two ways to teach the sit. One way is to place your dog on your left side with your right hand on his collar.

The left arm goes around his hindquarters tucking them under him while you say "Beau, sit." The other way is to pull up on his collar with your right hand while your left hand pushes down on his rump saying "Beau, sit." You will have to use your hands several times, maybe even for weeks, to enforce the sit position. Eventually he should learn to sit on command. When teaching the stay, you place your right hand in front of his face saying "stay" and walk away (leaving on your right foot) to the front of him and face him. In the beginning you will need to keep reminding him to stay and only leave for a few seconds, returning to him the way you left. Your beginning goal is to have him stay while you walk to the end of your 6-foot leash and the eventual goal is for him to stay for one minute

This is one way to train your dog to sit. The trainer's left arm is tucking the hindlegs in and her right hand is holding the collar.

off leash while you walk away and face him. When you return, it will be to his left and you go around behind his back to the heel position.

Down/Stay

The down is more difficult to teach but fortunately it is easier for small dogs, like Cockers, than the larger breeds. You will have your dog in the sit position on your left and say "Beau, down" while you reach over him with your left hand and grasp his left front leg. With your right hand, take his right front leg and pull both his legs forward. If he tries to get up, lean on his shoulder and encourage him to stay down. You can

relax him by stroking his back. Your goals are to get
him to go down on verbal command, and leave him by
first going to the front of him and eventually leaving
him for three minutes while standing 30 feet away.

Stand/Stay

The stand is even more difficult since
Cockers love to wiggle. This exercise is
important, not only for obedience and
conformation showing, but for
grooming and even for the
veterinarian's check up.

*When training it
is important that
the trainer has
the undivided
attention and eye
contact of the dog.*

In the obedience ring you are
allowed to manually pose your dog but it is nicer if
you can teach him to stand by walking him in to it.
The command is "Beau, stand," give a "stay" command
and again you leave on your right foot and walk to his
front. Return to him immediately. He needs to learn
to stand still while someone goes over him. For
instance, in obedience the judge will approach him
and touch him on his head, his middle and his rump.
In conformation the judge will do a more thorough
exam. It takes my dogs a while to learn to stand still
for the approach and exam. I have found it to be
helpful for some of those who are "wiggle worms" to
start with the sit. Have someone approach and touch
him. After graduating to the regular stand your goal is
to leave him 6 feet on leash and then 6 feet off leash.
Like the sit, you will return on his left and walk behind
him to the heel position. As you have noticed I use the
dog's name with the active command but not with the
"stay." Dogs learn to associate moving with hearing
their name.

Heeling

The definition of heeling is controlled walking at the
owner's left heel. It takes a long time to perfect this
exercise for the obedience ring. When you stop, the
dog is to sit automatically. It takes dedication to get

good heeling and automatic sits. The command is "Beau, heel," and you start off with your left foot. Did you notice that in the previous exercises you were to leave on your right foot? These are cues for your dog. The left foot means move and the right foot means he is to stay.

Your leash is in your right hand and your left hand is on it about half way down. Your left hand should be able to control the leash and there should be a little slack in it. The tight lead only strangles the dog. When there is slack you can give a little tug as necessary for corrections. Your dog should walk with you, with your leg somewhere between his nose and shoulder. Encourage him to stay with you, not forging (in front of you) or lagging behind you. When you come to a halt, be prepared physically to make him sit. Don't despair, coordination will come with experience.

TRAINING FOR OBEDIENCE TRIALS

The majority of our Cockers who are given the opportunity, thrive on obedience training and showing. If you would like to give it a try, you will need to seek help with an obedience club, although much of the advanced training is started at home. Good training books are available as well as obedience seminars given by experienced trainers. Today's training is based on attention (getting your dog to watch your every move) and keeping all training

This Cocker Spaniel is cooperating for the down command. Notice the position of the trainer's hands.

This Cocker Spaniel is practicing the stand exercise in the Novice class at an obedience trial. The judge would approach the dog and touch its head, middle of the back, and rump.

upbeat. One of the most important aspects of any kind of dog training is encouraging enthusiasm. In order for your dog to be enthusiastic, you must put on a good show for him. Sometimes you will feel rather ridiculous. It is important to put self consciousness out of your mind. Usually there is more than one way to train for an exercise. Perhaps you will need to experiment to see which way works best for your dog.

I start training my Cockers during puppyhood but find they aren't mature enough for obedience showing before the age of two. In the meantime we practice heeling (which can take many, many months to perfect and I might add that few of mine do perfect it) and dumbbell work around six to nine months of age, and jumping after the age of a year. Many trainers such

The definition of heeling is controlled walking at the handler's left side as demonstrated here. Note the eye contact.

as myself train a dog through CDX work before attempting to earn a CD.

Train and Treat

I showed my first Cocker in obedience in 1963. At that time the consensus of opinion was that our dogs should perform for the sheer pleasure of pleasing us. Using bait (food treats) was frowned on. As you will soon discover, most of our dogs are already a wee bit spoiled and therefore will respond more favorably when baited. I start by using food treats on young puppies to encourage them to come to me. It alleviates the "Catch me if you can" syndrome. I am partial to cooked liver to use as bait. I cook beef liver, cut it in small pieces, and put it in a plastic bag in the freezer. Of course you wouldn't want to give more than a small amount to prevent a GI upset. Liver is gobbled up much quicker than hard biscuits so you don't have to take time out for your dog to eat.

Read Your Dog

With some experience you will know when to use eye contact and when to avoid it. Personally, I seldom make eye contact with my Cockers when they are doing stay exercises. Usually I look to the side of them or over their heads. Some of my dogs are inclined to break their stays when I use eye contact. Also a few of my dogs have problems with eye contact when performing the recall. For some reason they don't come in all the way but sit out of reach about 3 feet away, which would be a failure at a show. If I look over the dog's head, then usually he comes in all the way. Learn how to read your dog's responses.

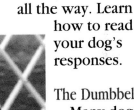

This Cocker sails over the high jump carrying a dumbbell. Make sure the dumbbell is the correct size for your dog.

The Dumbbell

Many dogs excel in the novice work, the handler agrees that this is great fun and decides to tackle CDX work. His dog quickly shows some aptitude for jumping but not for the hated dumbbell. Give some thought to teaching the dumbbell before or during the novice training. It usually takes me a long time to perfect this exercise and may hold me up going directly from the novice class into the open class. This slows down a good working dog that is at his prime for showing.

It is important to use the correct size dumbbell. You want the dumbbell wide enough for the Cocker's muzzle but not so wide as to allow play in it. The ends are tapered so the dog can see and the dowel is thick. Cockers don't like skinny dowels.

I teach the dumbbell by letting the dog hold it and carry it for a long time before I ask him to pick it up from the floor and eventually retrieve it. More often than not my dogs spit it out as soon as I put it in their mouths. When this happens I chuck them under the chin and say "hold it." Sometimes I have to hold my hand under the chin. After one or two seconds of holding it I say "out" and immediately take it. When they can hold it, and perhaps even do a sit/stay holding it, I try to encourage them to walk toward me with it and then heel with it. Frequently I have to hold his chin to keep him from spitting it out while walking with it. As you can see it takes patience. The next step is to lead him over the high jump (set low) carrying the dumbbell. At last I am ready for him to take it out of my hand and then pick it up off the floor.

Jumping

Cockers love to jump but I don't start them jumping until they are about a year old. I believe in preliminary hip x-rays before jumping. If you have an older Cocker that has shown any spinal problems, you probably shouldn't jump him. It would be all right to jump a young dog (under a year old) over an 8-inch board.

Most Cockers will jump 18 inches on the high jump and 36 inches over the broad jump. I start my dogs on leash over an 8-inch board, walking back and forth over it and circling around. This is the time to have him carry the dumbbell and start retrieving if he is ready. I gradually increase the height and may leave him on a sit/stay on one side while I walk over the jump (don't walk around it since he may follow your idea and go around too) then call him like a recall. I don't ask him to carry his dumbbell or retrieve it over his full height until he is reliable carrying, retrieving and jumping. Remember, treats will encourage him to perform dumbbell work and the jumps. Eventually you will want to proof him by throwing the dumbbell off center so he has to return over the jump from quite an angle.

I have always found the broad jump harder to teach than the high jump. My preference is to teach the high jump first to teach jumping high and making the necessary arc over it. A dog is supposed to lengthen his body and jump the broad jump flatter. When teaching this exercise first the dog may never properly make the necessary arc over the high jump and therefore hit it easier. When teaching the broad jump use your regular three boards but stand them on end and shorten the distance to perhaps 20 to 24 inches. Lead your dog over to it (whenever jumping a dog on a leash put him on the dead ring so not to choke him) several times and lengthen the jump with each session. When he is jumping satisfactorily you can lay one board down at a time. Go to the other side

When teaching the broad jump, keep in mind that your Cocker is supposed to lengthen his body and jump the broad jump flatter than the high jump.

of the jump and turn and face your dog and have him come over the jump like a recall. You can use a 15-foot lead if necessary. In time you can move from that position to the side of the jump (right angle to your dog) and send him. If he tries to avoid the jump, coming directly to you, lift your leg to block him. Frequently you have to vary back and forth between positions until he understands he is to jump.

Signals

This is a utility exercise but many trainers introduce signals at the novice level. Even if you never have intentions of showing in utility, this exercise has merit. There may be times in everyday life that signals will be useful and will be a requirement if your dog should ever lose his hearing, which is a distinct possibility later in life. It takes me a long time to prepare a dog for the signal exercise in the ring since they go through many stages from not wanting to perform or acknowledge they saw the hand signal (an attention problem in most cases) to wanting to please me through anticipation. Many trainers say anticipation is good but I find it difficult to correct in many exercises, probably because I do not take enough time to work through it.

During the signal exercise no verbal command is

given. Even the heeling is started with a hand signal. The dog heels on signal and then is expected to stand, drop, sit and come on signal.

I start my hand signals by teaching the drop:

The down signal. Raise the right hand and in the same motion the hand is returned to the side.

raising my right hand and in the same motion—not holding the hand up—the hand is returned to my side. The dog should drop before the hand is brought down. I work this on a 6-foot lead and initially stand very close, bringing my hand down gently on the dog's head. I like to give a treat when he cooperates. You gradually increase your distance and work towards faster drops, when your hand is going up. At the beginning you use the command "Beau, down" and wean him off the verbal command when he is dropping satisfactorily.

The signal to come. Take the right hand out perpendicular to the body and then bring it across the chest.

You can use either hand for the sit signal but I like to use my left hand. I stand in front of my dog bringing my hand up on the leash saying "Beau, sit." Give a treat when he sits and wean him off the verbal command while increasing your distance.

I give the signal to come with my right hand taking the hand out perpendicular to my body and then bringing it across my chest. In the beginning use your verbal command, "Beau, come" and signal on leash. Reward with a treat and eventually drop the verbal command.

You will need to work all signals close up on leash. Gradually increase your distance on leash, graduating to a distance of 40 to 50 feet off leash. Practice in strange places such as shopping centers. You need your dog's undivided attention to successfully perform signals.

Scent Discrimination

This is a very impressive exercise and one that takes time to teach, usually involving several relapses. The goal is for the dog to scent the correct article (the one with the handler's scent) among the four leather and four metal articles usually placed between the jumps or across the front of the ring. Sometimes they are placed in front of one of the jumps. I teach this exercise by tying down two to four articles on a piece of black rubber matting (such as would be in the ring). This exercise is done twice, once to seek the leather and then the metal, in either order. You need to air your article mat after tying down the articles for several days and during that time you can carry your practice articles in your pockets to start maximizing your scent. When teaching the exercise, some trainers use soft cheese on the

The goal of scent discrimination is for the dog to scent the correct article (the one with the handler's scent) among the four leather and four metal articles.

Lacey's Irish Cream, UDTX, shown here performing scent discrimination in the Utility class, ended up winning first place.

scented article. I rub liver on my hands and scent the article. This seems to sink in quicker for my dogs. Eventually you add more articles to the mat and then take them off the mat when your dog is doing them correctly. Don't be surprised if you have to go back to the mat. It is important to practice in different places, even shopping centers, and get other people to touch the unscented articles.

Directed Jumping

I consider the signal exercise and the go out part of the directed jumping to be the pitfalls of utility. The go outs and the directed jumping are taught as two separate exercises and are not combined until the dog has mastered them. I start the go outs by putting a target with a treat at the end of the ring and start my dog from about 6 feet on leash in front of it. I use my left hand, giving a signal, and then say "Beau, go out" and run him to the target. Let him get his treat and then tell him to sit. Many trainers use the dowel methods of teaching for the go outs. The dog is to find the dowel and return it to the handler. I have never used this method because many of my dogs will do the full go out only to turn and come in to me. It takes a lot of convincing to get them to sit out there and stay. I have felt the dowel method would further encourage their return to me. Perhaps my training lacks perseverance.

This is Ch. Sandor's Coming Attraction, UDTX, the first Cocker Spaniel to pass a TDX.

It is a good idea to teach the bar jump when teaching the high jump but this is not always convenient because of availability of jumps. This is a good time to suggest that you need to acquire a complete jump set: high, bar and broad. Your own set of jumps is important for training at different locations such as parking lots, school grounds, parks, shopping centers, etc. Your dog needs this experience.

Back to the directed jumping. Place your dog in front of the jump and say "Beau, hup" or whatever command you use. Hold your hand signal up at the same time and stay within 8 to 10 feet in front of the jump, depending on how cooperative your dog is. Usually my dogs are fine with the high jump but may need coaxing with the bar, perhaps even on lead. Your goal is to place your dog at greater angles and distance and you the same. This should be done very gradually. A few dogs have trouble gauging their take off from the greater distance so you shouldn't rush the training. Lately I have had a dog that is partial to one side or the other and it has been a difficult problem to correct. My best solution has been to avoid the verbal command and use only the hand signal.

One of the problems after introducing jumping is that he may be inclined to go out over the jumps.

Therefore, after my dog has learned his go outs and to go over the jumps I go back to the center of the ring to send him out to do the full exercise. As he gets more reliable I start backing up to the end of the ring. Sometimes there are relapses and I have to return to the center of the ring. Again it is important to train in many different areas. Presently I am working one dog that doesn't question go outs, which is rare, but she doesn't bother to look for the jumps in strange rings. Obviously it is going to take a lot of matches and different training sessions to get her to think about the jumps. Many dogs have accidents over the jumps and it is a real set back. They particularly dislike the clatter of the bar falling. Whenever your dog has an accident and is leery about jumping you need to lower the jump until he builds up his confidence.

I have not covered all the obedience exercises but only those that I find the most interesting. Much of your preliminary utility work will need to be started at home in a familiar environment until your dog is performing successfully. At that time you can gradually introduce him to exercises away from home. It is best in the advanced training to teach only one or two exercises at a time. Trying to teach too many exercises is too confusing.

I have found the utility class to be the most gratifying of all (except the tracking, which is my favorite dog

Cockers love to jump! Don't start them jumping until they are at least one year old.

activity). The bonding with the utility dog is incredible and never lost. Teaching and earning the title doesn't come easy. I shouldn't admit this, but I had one dog take four years with one year off while I was contemplating giving up. He had a terrible go out problem refusing to go past the jumps where he felt secure. However, at matches and training sessions he passed with flying colors.

Most Cockers will jump 18 inches on the high jump. It is important that they are taught to make the necessary arc over it.

Eventually he gained his confidence. I am glad I didn't give up.

I have known several Cockers that have earned their UD's after the age of ten, which says a lot for the health and stamina of the breed. It takes a dog that is sound of mind and body to finish a UD since it doesn't come easily to most. Many years ago it was nicknamed "futility" and we still have reason to call it that. So many different things can go wrong in the ring, and it doesn't take long for a dog to realize he can get away with it again the next time out. Is it worth it to train the geriatric dog? I think so as long as the dog is in good health. Just recently I finished a CDX on a seven-year-old who knows nothing about utility, but I am going to give it a try. It will take me at least 12 to 18 months to train her so Father Time may cheat us, but as long as she is willing, then so am I.

I will never have the perseverance or patience to train for an OTCh but I am very proud of those who have succeeded with their Cockers. They should be commended. Years ago, prior to today's so-called super breeds, Cockers placed very well in competition. Presently, I see more dedication to training and their performances are improving. Those few handlers who have succeeded earning UDXs and OTChs are upholding the reputation of the Cocker in obedience. I hope I have encouraged some of you to enjoy your Cocker in the obedience ring.

TRACKING

This is my favorite dog activity. There is nothing more wonderful than watching a dog using his nose and scenting out the track. I like to start my Cockers after they earn their CDXs, feeling it is a change of pace before the tedious utility training. I also feel it helps with the scent discrimination and the go outs since the dog needs to work at least 20 feet in front of you. I don't like to start tracking any earlier because it does encourage them to put their noses to the ground which sometimes is already a problem for Cockers. (Along this line, never let your Cocker sniff at a show. It's a bad habit that can carry over to the ring.) I feel intensive utility training inhibits the urge to track so that is another reason why I start after the CDX.

I start my Cockers on a liver track, which involves rubbing liver on the bottom of my boots every few paces. Liver quickly encourages them to put their noses to the ground. Put a dowel in the ground, scuff your feet a little and walk in a straight line towards a land marker such as a tree, bush, utility pole, etc. At the end of your track put your article down with a piece of liver under it. Your dog will have to dig at the article (indicating it) to get the treat. In a test the dog only has to indicate the article, not retrieve it. Usually I try three short, straight tracks (trying to change the wind direction with each track) on the first day double laying them, which means I return over my original track. Depending on my dog I may be able to introduce a wide angle turn on the second or third session. In the beginning, while I am laying my tracks I like to leave my dog in his harness tied to a fence or tree just a few feet from the start of the track. By the time I return he has a good whiff of the liver and is anxious to start.

Some handlers like to down their dog at the starting flag but I prefer my dog to be tracking (following the tracklayer's path to the flag) when he reaches the start and let him keep on tracking. In my opinion, most dogs do track up to the flag and you are only disrupting him by putting his harness on or downing him.

I do believe in occasional food drops and liver on the feet to get a dog interested, but I try to wean him as soon as possible. I have a problem with too many food drops since my dogs tend to be more interested in the food then in learning about tracking. I always put a piece of liver under the glove and sometimes will put down extra gloves, or articles, with treats as a reward for committing to a turn. I use these rewards about 30 yards past the turn. I have found that occasionally my dogs make good indication of loss of track and indicate the turn but then chicken out of committing to it. Rewards help.

There is nothing more wonderful than watching a Cocker using his nose and scenting out the track.

You build up your age, length and turns gradually. Find a tracking buddy to help because after your dog is tracking you will need to start him on blind

tracks. It is important that you (when you lay down your tracks) and your tracklayer always know where the track is. I like to use colored clothes pins and markers on legs and turns, but if I have a tracklayer then I want him to hide my markers. I tend to use them as crutches.

Agility is an obstacle course designed to test a dog's intelligence and coordination. Many Cocker Spaniels show a love and natural ability for it.

When starting a dog I like to go out three days in a row, with a day off in between, until he gets the idea. If all goes well and your dog shows natural ability, you may be ready for a tracking test in about six months although I had one pass 60 days after she started to track. Unfortunately her TDX work will take much longer than usual because she really doesn't have much tracking experience. I like my T dogs to be started on X work before they get their T's. Obviously I have written only a few of my tips so you will have to read some books and perhaps enroll in a tracking class or attend a seminar. Give it a try—the exercise is great for both of you.

AGILITY

Agility is off and running in the U.S. and dog owners are loving every minute of it. Many Cockers show a love and natural ability for it. Unfortunately I have not been able to compete because of my health. My bad knee and bad back will not allow me to run with my dog. I have practiced some agility obstacles with a couple of my dogs and they were thrilled with the fun and excitement of it all. Agility does relieve stress and surely builds confidence, not only in the dog but for the handler/dog team.

This Cocker Spaniel is clearing the bar jump at an agility trial.

You can start puppies on the smaller obstacles, but for competition training your dog should have some obedience training and be able to perform off leash. The major problem with agility is trying to find courses to train over. The equipment takes up a lot of room and it is quite time consuming to break down and put up a course. Many hands are needed.

HUNTING

Cocker Spaniels are members of the Sporting Group and therefore should be able to perform in the hunting field, but very few of them do. There has been renewed interest in hunting, not only for Cockers but also for the other Sporting breeds. Hunting is in. If you wish to give it a try, you should get professional help, which may be hard to find. The flushing spaniels do not perform the same way as Golden Retrievers or Labradors, etc. They must learn to quarter the field, flush game and retrieve it. The JH, SH and MH tests become progressively more difficult. You may want to look up some English Cocker or English Springer folks in your area. They may be able to point you in the right direction for help.

The Cocker Spaniel is a natural hunter and retriever both on land and in the water. Practice retrieving with a dummy such as this one.

In closing I can only hope that I have enlightened you to what a Cocker is capable of doing. You can enhance your relationship with some basic training that will be invaluable throughout his life. If your only desire is to have a faithful companion dog, you have chosen the right breed. I can only hope that you enjoy your Cocker half as much as I have enjoyed mine.

This Cocker Spaniel is lined out for a retrieve, which means that the handler is pointing him in the direction of the game.

GROOMING Your Cocker Spaniel

When prospective buyers call me for information about Cockers, the first thing I point out is the necessity of regular grooming. It isn't fair to the breed to ignore the importance of routine grooming for good health, but also one shouldn't hide the Cocker Spaniel's beauty. With regularly scheduled groomings at least every six to eight weeks (more often if you have the time) a Cocker can be relatively easy to keep. In addition, it is a good idea to plan on at least a quick weekly comb-out, which can be accomplished in 15 to 20 minutes while you're watching TV.

Grooming sessions can be a special time for owners to spend with their Cockers. If made pleasant, your Cocker Spaniel will look forward to these bonding opportunities.

Many breeds, including mixed breeds, need similar care. Yes, Cockers do shed but their hair is easily vacuumed. Several years ago I owned a short-haired breed and found it nearly impossible to vacuum the hair off the sofa and chairs. It was awful.

Grooming is a special time I spend with my Cockers. It gives me the opportunity to do my "at home physical" and perhaps find something that needs to be brought to my veterinarian's attention. Even if you have your Cocker professionally groomed try to remember to check him over when you brush or comb him between groomings. A good groomer will point out obvious abnormalities.

EQUIPMENT

You will find some type of grooming table, either the real thing or a card table, picnic table, etc., a necessity. Dogs behave so much better when they cannot avoid the situation by running off. It won't take long to train your

dog to stay on the table and very likely the breeder has already table-trained him. The table will save your back as well as prevent you from having to get down on your hands and knees and coax your Cocker to stay put.

You need a good set of clippers and a #10 blade to get started. Later you may want to add a #7 for trimming the back and a #15 for closer trimming of the face. Other equipment needed is a comb, straight shears, a pair of single-sided thinning scissors, nail trimmer, pin brush and a slicker brush. If you wish to purchase your equipment a little bit at a time, you can start with the clipper and #10 blade, comb, nail trimmer and a pair of straight shears.

TRIMMING

Everyone can learn to trim their Cocker Spaniels and there is an advantage if owners learn to do it themselves. Not only will it save money over the years but owners can trim more frequently, which will keep their Cockers happier. Trimming is much easier on the dog when it is done every four to six weeks. Ask your breeder to give you some instruction or if this isn't possible, try to trim your dog about three to four weeks after his last trimming. You will be able to follow the pattern left by the last grooming. Many owners express concern about a poor trim or injuring the dog. It is next to impossible to injure him when using clippers but a good possibility when cutting out a mat with scissors. Remember the hair will always grow back and you will have the opportunity to perfect your skills.

I usually start on the ear, about one-third down at the flap, and use the #10 blade going up against the hair. At the top of the ear, when meeting the skull, you need to lift the clipper a little so as not to dig in and leave a ridge. Next you trim the underneath side of the ear, trimming closely around the ear canal. It is important to keep the hair trimmed close in this area, particularly if you are medicating the ear.

Next I start on the muzzle, trimming against the hair with a #10 or a #15 blade. Be sure to trim closely around the eyes and lip folds. Many Cockers' eyes tear (because of tear duct problems or distichiasis) and the area can become inflamed when the hair is left too long. This is an area you might want to trim up in between regular groomings. Some Cockers have serious problems with lip fold infections so it is helpful to keep this area trimmed as short as possible. Again you may need to do "touch ups" in between groomings. Both of these areas may need periodic washings; the eyes with warm water and the lip folds with soap and water. Don't neglect the eyelashes and whiskers. Cockers are Sporting dogs and shouldn't look like Bambi.

A sad looking Cocker Spaniel, Jessica, definitely needs a grooming...

A Cocker's skull is to be rounded and not flat, although we do see flat skulls. With careful trimming you can give a rounded look to most Cocker Spaniels. I start with the back half of the skull and use the #10 blade trimming with the hair back to the top of the neck. This area is trimmed short. I use thinning scissors on the front half of the skull trying to give the appearance of a rounded skull. Take off a little bit at a time, thinning the hair until it lays flat. Blend the edges to the sides of the skull and into the back half. It takes some work to give it a pleasing look. Again more frequent trimmings will be helpful since his "top knot" tends to grow out and become unmanageable, affecting the next hair cut. Some dogs have cowlicks, which make grooming even more interesting.

After trimming the ears and the skull I go to the underneath part of the neck, taking the #10 or the #15 blade against the hair. This can be a sensitive area but I have found there is little problem when the hair has not grown too long. If it is very long, then it is necessary to shorten slowly by taking the blade with the hair and then returning with the clipper against the hair. This should prevent irritation. If there is any irritation in this area or around the ears, try using an over-the-counter antibiotic steroid ointment for a few days. This is commonly called a "clipper burn" or a "hot spot" and can happen to the best of groomers and dogs. Those dogs prone to staph infections are particularly susceptible.

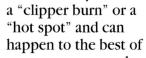

Use thinning scissors on the front half of the skull to give the appearance of a rounded skull. Take off a little bit at a time, thinning the hair until it lays flat.

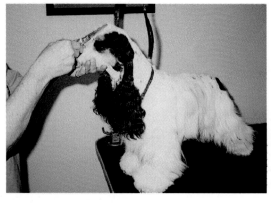

After trimming the underneath part of the neck, I trim the sides of the neck, with a #10 blade going with the hair down to the point of the shoulder. On pet Cockers the top of the neck and back can be trimmed, with the #7 blade or #10 blade if the former is not available, gently going with the hair. The #7 leaves the coat longer than the #10. Don't use a clipper on the backs of show dogs. Some groomers and owners tend to take the sides down low leaving only a fringe of side coat. They usually shave the belly. This type of cut may be necessary on the dog that mats easily (which frequently happens after spaying or neutering) and is basically a carefree cut. Not much combing is required. The tail is trimmed clean with thinning scissors.

A beautiful Jessica after a full grooming session. Your Cocker should have regularly scheduled groomings every six to eight weeks.

Trim the nails before trimming the feet. Some Cockers can be real wimps during the routine nail trim. Be kind to your dog by making sure your nail trimmers are sharp. Dull nail trimmers are painful and can ruin a good dog. If you should "quick" a nail (cut too short), try sticking the nail in a cake of soft soap. That should stop the bleeding. If your dog misbehaves during nail trimming have someone restrain him and under no circumstances let him free until you are finished trimming the nails. When you let your dog get away with it, each time he will continually struggle and for longer periods until he gets his way.

The next step is to trim the hair on the bottom of the feet even with the pads. Check between the toes for mats and interdigital cysts. Usually mats aren't a problem when

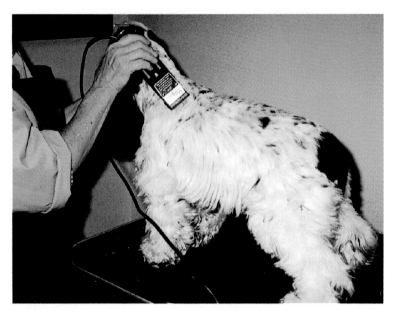

When trimming the back, use the #10 or #7 blade and cut with the hair.

you trim frequently. After that shorten and round the hair on the top of the foot.

I like to use the #10 blade to clean out the underside of the elbows, which is an area that mats easily. Comb out the legs and decide how much you are going to take off. "A puppy cut" leaves the hair about 2 inches long. Show people are layering the feathering on the legs starting with the feet and working up. If you decide to try this you may want to study some photos of show Cockers to get a better idea. It is no longer fashionable for the show Cocker to have a coat hanging to the floor so the legs are layered and the side coat is shaped. More than likely this is not a concern for you since the majority of pet owners elect the more carefree cut.

EARS

Grooming is the perfect time to examine the ears and clean them thoroughly before the bath. It is best to do this after the hair is trimmed short around the ears. Cockers are prone to ear infections, which may be secondary to an underlying condition such as hypothyroidism or allergies. If your dog has recurrent infections, then the source needs to be investigated.

It is handy to keep a little squirt bottle with a mixture of 50 percent white vinegar and 50 percent water or a mixture of three percent hydrogen peroxide and 70 percent Isopropyl alcohol. I like to squirt this in the ears and wipe them out with cotton balls. When using cotton tip applicators you must be cautious not to pack debris down into the ear canal and create more problems. Under no circumstances should you allow any water to run into the ears. You may be able to avoid this by putting cotton balls in the ears when bathing. It is a good idea to apply a drying agent in the ears after bathing.

Clean up the tail with thinning scissors. Do not leave feathers on the tail.

THE BATH

You need to get organized with your shampoo, bath towels, hair dryer and make sure the house is warm (especially for young puppies) and draft free. If you are bathing in between groomings, be sure to comb out any mats first otherwise they will be impossible to get out after the bath. It is a good idea to take your dog out for a quick potty trip since he may get excited and need to go but won't be able to go until he is thoroughly dried. Damp skin may lead to "hot spots" or a sick puppy.

Years ago frequent bathing was not recommended but attitudes have changed. In my opinion young puppies need to be bathed at least every two weeks if not every week. They get dirty so quickly. Show dogs get bathed at least weekly with a good conditioning shampoo. Usually I try to bathe my house dogs every two to three weeks. It takes work but the results are a clean dog and a respectable coat. I think the coat mats easier when it is dirty. In my opinion frequent bathings contribute to healthier skin because it keeps down the growth of bacteria on the skin.

You should use a good grooming or conditioning shampoo that will not dry out the skin. I am a firm believer in refraining from medicated shampoos unless they are prescribed by your veterinarian. Remember some medicated shampoos are not to be used permanently and are occasionally changed to a different type of medicated shampoo. On those dogs with skin problems it may be necessary to use a couple of shampoos on different areas of the skin.

If your dog has fleas, you should use a good flea shampoo and start with the neck, lathering a ring around it to prevent fleas from rushing to the top of the head. After that, work your way back and let it sit on the dog for the recommended time.

I like to use bath time to express the anal sacs so you can wash the odor away. After bathing, towel thoroughly and then brush your dog while using the hair dryer. Few dogs care for the "little monster" but they all learn to tolerate it.

The Cocker Spaniel is a proud dog that deserves to look like one—not a woolly teddy bear. Cocker owners are also proud and the majority of them take excellent care of their pets, which contributes to better health and attitude. A groomed Cocker is a pleasure to behold.

MORE ON EARS

Ear disease is a common, frustrating condition in Cocker Spaniels. It is important to understand the factors that lead to ear disease and the problems that cause it to persist. A simple method for understanding ear disease is the three P's: predisposing, primary, and perpetuating.

Predisposing causes of ear disease include: hair filled ear canals, moisture from high humidity, bathing or swimming, and stenosis. Stenosis refers to the ear canal becoming smaller due to swelling and inflammation. Some dogs may be born with a small ear canal, which predisposes them to ear disease. Other predisposing causes may include increased numbers and increased size of glands in the ear canal. This occurs commonly in Cocker Spaniels. Pendulous pinna and ear canals that have been over medicated may also lead to ear disease.

Use the hair dryer with the brush for drying and fluffing the coat. (Do you notice this Cocker's undocked tail?)

Primary causes of ear disease are often overlooked when diagnosing and treating ear disease. One of the best examples is allergic ear disease. Cocker Spaniels with atopy (inhaled allergies) or food allergy will often initially develop reddened, inflamed ears that cause itching and head shaking. (They don't always have to itch.) If the affected ear is untreated, bacterial and yeast infections will develop. To resolve the otitis, the allergies must be diagnosed and managed. Other primary causes of ear disease include: primary seborrhea; endocrine diseases, such as hypothyroidism; demodicosis; scabies; ear mites; and auto-immune diseases, such as pemphigus foliaceous.

The last of the P's are the perpetuating factors, these are factors that cause the ear disease to continue even if the other two P's have been addressed. Perpetuating factors include bacterial infections, yeast infections and middle ear infections. The bacterial and yeast infections are commonly diagnosed and treated, but if the predisposing and primary factors are not diagnosed and treated, the infections will be recurrent and resistant to treatment.

Your veterinarian may recommend sedating your dog and flushing the ears. I have had success using a solution containing dioctyl sodium sulfosuccinate, carbamide peroxide and tetracaine. This solution is applied before the flushing and excels at loosening the debris. The process may need to be done several times until the infection is under control. There is little value in treating dirty ears since the medication cannot come in contact with the ear canal. Your veterinarian may recommend that you return at least every two weeks for a recheck until the infection is gone. If the infection recurs again in the near future, or becomes chronic, then your veterinarian may suggest further testing and/or perhaps a hypoallergenic diet on a trial basis for ten to 12 weeks. He may refer you to a dermatologist.

If ears are not properly cared for, they may become a surgical case sometime in the future. It is interesting to note that usually both ears are afflicted, but occasionally only one ear may be involved. Do have your veterinarian explain proper ear maintenance before there is a problem.

SEBORRHEA

Unfortunately some Cockers are afflicted with

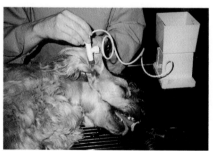

seborrhea. Seborrhea refers to increased scale and sebum production from the skin. Seborrhea can be greasy

Your veterinarian may recommend sedating your Cocker and flushing the ears with a Water Pik.

(oleosa) or dry (sicca). Another method to define seborrhea is primary versus secondary. Secondary seborrhea can be caused by various conditions including allergic disease, bacterial skin infections and thyroid disease. The list of causes for secondary seborrhea is extensive because any disease that causes the skin to produce more sebum or skin cells may lead to secondary seborrhea.

Primary seborrhea is a condition recognized in several breeds with the Cocker being affected most commonly. This is similar to secondary seborrhea in that the skin cells and sebum are being over produced. Unlike secondary seborrhea, the reason for the over production is from a defect in the skin and sebaceous gland cells. Affected dogs are born with this cellular defect.

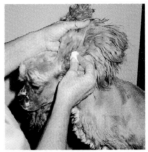

Use a cotton ball to wipe out your Cocker's ears. Do not stick anything into your dog's ears.

It is difficult to differentiate between primary and secondary seborrhea. Cocker Spaniels with either form will have recurrent ear infections and dry or greasy scaling especially of the neck and trunk. They will also commonly develop recurrent bacterial skin infections, which may create an offensive odor. Fortunately, there are a number of therapies including medicated baths and oral medications. Some Cocker Spaniels with primary seborrhea will respond with high daily doses of vitamin A. These vitamin A responsive seborrheas are not due to a deficiency of vitamin A. They improve because of a pharmacologic dosage of vitamin A. The correct dosage of vitamin A should be administered only under your veterinarian's guidance.

(The above information pertaining to ear disease and seborrhea was contributed by Dr. John Gordon, MedVet, Columbus, OH, Board Certified Dermatologist.)

SPORT of Purebred Dogs

Welcome to the exciting and sometimes frustrating sport of dogs. No doubt you are trying to learn more about dogs or you wouldn't be deep into this book. This section covers the basics that may entice you, further your knowledge and help you to understand the dog world. If you decide to give showing, obedience or any other dog activities a try, then I suggest you seek further help from the appropriate source.

Dog showing has been a very popular sport for a long time and has been taken quite seriously by some. Others only enjoy it as a hobby.

The Kennel Club in England was formed in 1859, the American Kennel Club was established in 1884 and the Canadian Kennel Club was formed in 1888. The purpose of these clubs was to register purebred dogs and maintain their Stud Books. In the beginning, the concept of registering dogs was not readily accepted. More than 36 million dogs have been enrolled in the AKC Stud Book since its inception in 1888. Presently the kennel clubs not only register dogs but adopt and enforce rules and regulations governing dog shows, obedience trials and field trials. Over the years they have fostered and encouraged interest in the health and welfare of the purebred dog.

This is Katherine of Emerald Eire, UDT, WD, earning her Utility Dog title at 10 years of age. Owners, Pat and Dan Brannan.

They routinely donate funds to veterinary research for study on genetic disorders.

Below are the addresses of the kennel clubs in the United States, Great Britain and Canada.

The American Kennel Club
51 Madison Avenue
New York, NY 10010
(Their registry is located at: 5580 Centerview Drive, STE 200, Raleigh, NC 27606-3390)

The Kennel Club
1 Clarges Street
Piccadilly, London, WIY 8AB, England

The Canadian Kennel Club
111 Eglinton Avenue
East Toronto, Ontario M6S 4V7
Canada

Conformation showing is our oldest dog sport. It is based on the dog's appearance—his structure, movement, and attitude.

Today there are numerous activities that are enjoyable for both the dog

and the handler. Some of the activities include conformation showing, obedience competition, tracking, agility, the Canine Good Citizen Certificate, and a wide range of instinct tests that vary from breed to breed. Where you start depends upon your goals which early on may not be readily apparent.

CONFORMATION

Conformation showing is our oldest dog show sport. This type of showing is based on the dog's appearance—that is his structure, movement and attitude. When considering this type of showing, you need to be aware of your breed's standard and be able to evaluate your dog compared to that standard. The breeder of your puppy or other experienced breeders would be good sources for such an evaluation. Puppies can go through lots of changes over a period of time. I always say most puppies start out as promising hopefuls and then after maturing may be disappointing as show candidates. Even so this should not deter them from being excellent pets.

When considering conformation showing, you need to be aware of your breed's standard and be able to evaluate your dog compared to that standard.

Usually conformation training classes are offered by the local kennel or obedience clubs. These are excellent places for training puppies. The puppy should be able to walk on a lead before entering such a class. Proper ring procedure and technique for posing (stacking) the dog will be demonstrated as well as gaiting the dog. Usually certain patterns are used in the ring such as the triangle or the "L." Conformation class, like the PKT class, will give your youngster the opportunity to socialize with different breeds of dogs and humans too.

It takes some time to learn the routine of conformation showing. Usually one starts at the puppy matches which may be AKC Sanctioned or Fun Matches. These matches are generally for puppies from two or three months to a year old, and there may be classes for the adult over the age of 12 months. Similar to point shows, the classes are divided by sex and after completion of the classes in that breed or variety, the class

A show dog must be trained to stand while a judge examines him.

winners compete for Best of Breed or Variety. The winner goes on to compete in the Group and the Group winners compete for Best in Match. No championship points are awarded for match wins.

A few matches can be great training for puppies even though there is no intention to go on showing. Matches enable the puppy to meet new people and be handled by a stranger—the judge. It is also a change of environment, which broadens the horizon for both dog and handler. Matches and other dog activities boost the confidence of the handler and especially the younger handlers.

Earning an AKC championship is built on a point system, which is different from Great Britain. To become an AKC Champion of Record the dog must earn 15 points. The number of points earned each time depends upon the number of dogs in competition. The number of points available at each show depends upon the breed, its sex and the location of the show. The United States is divided into ten AKC zones. Each zone has its own set of points. The purpose of the zones is to try to equalize the points available from breed to breed and area to area. The AKC adjusts the point scale annually.

The number of points that can be won at a show are between one and five. Three-, four- and five-point wins are considered majors. Not only does the dog need 15 points won under three different judges, but those points must include two majors under two different judges. Canada also works on a point system but majors are not required.

Junior Showmanship

The Junior Showmanship Class is a wonderful way to build self confidence even if there are no aspirations of staying with the dog-show game later in life. Frequently, Junior Showmanship becomes the background of those who become successful exhibitors/handlers in the future. In some instances it is taken very seriously, and success is measured in terms of wins. The Junior Handler is judged solely on his ability and skill in presenting his dog. The dog's conformation is not to be considered by the judge. Even so the condition and grooming of the dog may be a reflection upon the handler.

CANINE GOOD CITIZEN

The AKC sponsors a program to encourage dog owners to train their dogs. Local clubs perform the pass/fail tests, and dogs who pass are awarded a Canine Good Citizen

The Westminster Kennel Club Dog Show is the most prestigious in the United States. It is held in New York City annually.

Certificate. Proof of vaccination is required at the time of participation. The test includes:
1. Accepting a friendly stranger.
2. Sitting politely for petting.
3. Appearance and grooming.
4. Walking on a loose leash.
5. Walking through a crowd.
6. Sit and down on command/staying in place.
7. Come when called.
8. Reaction to another dog.
9. Reactions to distractions.
10. Supervised separation.

If more effort was made by pet owners to accomplish these exercises, fewer dogs would be cast off to the humane shelter.

Ringside at the Ohio Valley Cocker Spaniel Club Specialty Show. For many exhibitors, the challenge lies at specialty shows.

OBEDIENCE

Obedience is necessary, without a doubt, but it can also become a wonderful hobby or even an obsession. In my opinion, obedience classes and competition can provide wonderful

companionship, not only with your dog but with your classmates or fellow competitors. It is always gratifying to discuss your dog's problems with others who have had similar experiences. The AKC acknowledged Obedience around 1936, and it has changed tremendously even though many of the exercises are basically the same. Today, obedience competition is just that—very competitive. Even so, it is possible for every obedience exhibitor to come home a winner (by earning qualifying scores) even though he/she may not earn a placement in the class.

TRACKING

Tracking is officially classified obedience, but I feel it should have its own category. There are three tracking titles available: Tracking Dog (TD), Tracking Dog Excellent (TDX), Variable Surface Tracking (VST). If all three tracking titles are obtained, then the dog officially becomes a CT (Champion Tracker). The CT will go in front of the dog's name.

A TD may be earned anytime and does not have to follow the other obedience titles. There are many exhibitors that prefer tracking to obedience, and there are others like myself that do both. In my experience with small dogs, I prefer to earn the CD and CDX before attempting tracking. My reasoning is that small dogs are closer to the mat in the obedience rings and therefore it's

Agility is a fascinating sport that the dog, handler and spectators enjoy to the utmost. Agility is a spectator sport!

too easy to put the nose down and sniff. Tracking encourages sniffing. Of course this depends on the dog. I've had some dogs that tracked around the ring and others (TDXs) who wouldn't think of sniffing in the ring.

The broad jump is one exercise in open obedience. Today obedience competition is just that—very competitive.

AGILITY

Agility was first introduced by John Varley in England at the Crufts Dog Show, February 1978, but Peter Meanwell, competitor and judge, actually developed the idea. It was officially recognized in the early '80s. Agility is extremely popular in England and Canada and growing in popularity in the U.S. The AKC acknowledged agility in August 1994. Dogs must be at least 12 months of age to be entered. It is a fascinating sport that the dog, handler and spectators enjoy to the utmost. Agility is a spectator sport! The dog performs off lead. The handler either runs with his dog or positions himself on the course and directs his dog with verbal and hand signals over a timed course over or through a variety of obstacles including a time out or pause. One of the main drawbacks to agility is finding a place to train. The obstacles take up a lot of space and it is very time consuming to put up and take down courses.

PERFORMANCE TESTS

During the last decade the American Kennel Club has promoted performance tests—those events that test the different breeds' natural abilities. This type of event encourages a handler to devote even more time to his dog and retain the natural instincts of his breed heritage. It is an important part of the wonderful world of dogs.

Hunting Titles

For retrievers, pointing breeds and spaniels. Titles offered are Junior Hunter (JH), Senior Hunter (SH), and Master Hunter (MH).

Flushing Spaniels Their primary purpose is to hunt, find, flush and return birds to hand as quickly as possible in a pleasing and obedient manner. The entrant must be at least six months of age and dogs with limited registration (ILP) are eligible. Game used are pigeons, pheasants, and quail.

Retrievers Limited registration (ILP) retrievers are not eligible to compete in Hunting Tests. The purpose of a Hunting Test for retrievers is to test the merits of and evaluate the abilities of retrievers in the field in order to determine their suitability and ability as hunting companions. They are expected to retrieve any type of game bird, pheasants, ducks, pigeons, guinea hens and quail.

Pointing Breeds Are eligible at six months of age, and dogs with limited registration (ILP) are permitted. They must show a keen desire to hunt; be bold and independent; have a fast, yet attractive, manner of hunting; and demonstrate intelligence not only in seeking objectives but also in the ability to find game. They must establish point, and in the more advanced tests they need to be steady to wing and must remain in position until the bird is shot or they are released.

A Senior Hunter must retrieve. A Master Hunter must honor. The judges and the marshal are permitted to ride horseback during the test

General Information

Obedience, tracking and agility allow the purebred dog with an Indefinite Listing Privilege (ILP) number or a limited registration to be exhibited and earn titles. Application must be made to the AKC for an ILP number.

The American Kennel Club publishes a monthly *Events* magazine that is part of the *Gazette*, their official journal for the sport of purebred dogs. The *Events* section lists upcoming shows and the secretary or superintendent for them. The majority of the conformation shows in the U.S. are overseen by licensed superintendents. Generally the entry closing date is approximately two-and-a-half weeks before the actual show. Point shows are fairly expensive, while the match shows cost about one third of the point show entry fee. Match shows usually take entries the day of the show but some are pre-entry. The best way to find match show information is through your local kennel club. Upon asking, the AKC can provide you with a list of superintendents, and you can write and ask to be put on their mailing lists.

Obedience trial and tracking test information is available through the AKC. Frequently these events are not superintended, but put on by the host club. Therefore you would make the entry with the event's secretary.

As you have read, there are numerous activities you can share with your dog. Regardless what you do, it does take teamwork. Your dog can only benefit from your attention and training. I hope this chapter has enlightened you and hope, if nothing else, you will attend a show here and there. Perhaps you will start with a puppy kindergarten class, and who knows where it may lead!

The primary purpose of flushing spaniels, such as the Cocker, is to hunt, find, flush and return birds to hand as quickly as possible. This Cocker retrieves a pigeon in training.

DENTAL CARE for Your Dog's Life

So you've got a new puppy! You also have a new set of puppy teeth in your household. Anyone who has ever raised a puppy is abundantly aware of these new teeth. Your puppy will chew anything it can reach, chase your shoelaces, and play "tear the rag" with any piece of clothing it can find. When puppies are newly born, they have no teeth. At about four weeks of age, puppies of most breeds begin to develop their deciduous or baby teeth. They begin eating semi-solid food, fighting and biting with their litter mates, and learning discipline from their mother. As their new teeth come in, they inflict more pain on their mother's breasts, so her feeding sessions become less frequent and shorter. By six or eight weeks, the mother will start growling to warn her pups when they are fighting too roughly or hurting her as they nurse too much with their new teeth.

Puppies need to chew. It is a necessary part of their physical and mental development. They develop muscles and necessary life skills as they drag objects around, fight over possession, and vocalize alerts and warnings. Puppies chew on things to explore their world. They are using their sense of taste to determine what is food and what is not. How else can they tell an electrical cord from a lizard? At about four months of age, most puppies begin shedding their baby teeth. Often these teeth need some help to come out and make way for the permanent teeth. The incisors (front teeth) will be replaced first. Then, the adult canine or fang teeth erupt. When the baby tooth is not shed before the permanent tooth comes in, veterinarians call it a retained deciduous tooth. This condition will often cause gum infections by trapping hair and debris between the permanent tooth and the retained baby tooth. Nylafloss® is an excellent device for puppies to use. They can toss it, drag it, and chew on the many surfaces it presents. The baby teeth can catch in the nylon material, aiding in their removal. Puppies that have adequate chew toys will have less destructive behavior, develop more physically, and have less chance of retained deciduous teeth.

During the first year, your dog should be seen by your

veterinarian at regular intervals. Your veterinarian will let you know when to bring in your puppy for vaccinations and parasite examinations. At each visit, your veterinarian should inspect the lips, teeth, and mouth as part of a complete physical examination. You should take some part in the maintenance of your dog's oral health. You should examine your dog's mouth weekly throughout his first year to make sure there are no sores, foreign objects, tooth problems, etc. If your dog drools excessively, shakes its head, or has bad breath, consult your veterinarian. By the time your dog is six months old, the permanent teeth are all in and plaque can start to accumulate on the tooth surfaces. This is when your dog needs to develop good dental-care habits to prevent calculus build-up on its teeth. Brushing is best. That is a fact that cannot be denied. However, some dogs do not like their teeth brushed regularly, or you may not be able to accomplish the task. In that case, you should consider a product that will help prevent plaque and calculus build-up.

The nylon tug toy is actually dental floss. Do NOT use cotton rope tug toys as cotton is organic and rots.

The Plaque Attackers® and Galileo Bone® are other excellent choices for the first three years of a dog's life. Their shapes make them interesting for the dog. As the dog chews on them, the solid polyurethane massages the gums which improves the blood circulation to the periodontal tissues. Projections on the chew devices increase the surface and are in contact with the tooth for more efficient cleaning. The unique shape and consistency prevent your dog from exerting excessive force on his own teeth or from breaking off pieces of the bone. If your dog is an aggressive chewer or weighs more than 55 pounds (25 kg), you should consider giving him a Nylabone®, the most durable chew product on the market.

The Gumabones ®, made by the Nylabone Company, are constructed of strong polyurethane, which is softer than nylon.

Less powerful chewers prefer the Gumabones® to the Nylabones®. A super option for your dog is the Hercules Bone®, a uniquely shaped bone named after the great Olympian for its exceptional strength. Like all Nylabone products, they are specially scented to make them attractive to your dog. Ask your veterinarian about these bones and he will validate the good doctor's prescription: Nylabones® not only give your dog a good chewing workout but also help to save your dog's teeth (and even his life, as it protects him from possible fatal periodontal diseases).

By the time dogs are four years old, 75% of them have periodontal disease. It is the most common infection in dogs. Yearly examinations by your veterinarian are essential to maintaining your dog's good health. If your veterinarian detects periodontal disease, he or she may recommend a prophylactic cleaning. To do a thorough cleaning, it will be necessary to put your dog under anesthesia. With modern gas anesthetics and monitoring equipment, the procedure is safe. Your veterinarian will scale the teeth with an ultrasound scaler or hand instrument. This removes the calculus from the teeth. If there are calculus deposits below the gum line, the veterinarian will plane the roots to make them smooth. After all of the calculus has been removed, the teeth are polished with pumice in a polishing cup. If any medical or surgical

A super option for your dog is the Hercules® by Nylabone®, a uniquely shaped bone named after the great Olympian for its exceptional strength.

treatment is needed, it is done at this time. The final step would be fluoride treatment and your follow-up treatment at home. If the periodontal disease is advanced, the veterinarian may prescribe a medicated mouth rinse or antibiotics for use at home. Make sure your dog has safe, clean and attractive chew toys and treats. Chooz® treats are another way of using a consumable treat to help keep your dog's teeth clean.

Pet shops sell dog treats that are healthy and nutritious. Cheese is added to chicken meal and other high-protein feeds to be melted together and molded into hard chew devices.

Rawhide is the most popular of all materials for a dog to chew. This has never been good news to dog owners, because rawhide is inherently very dangerous for dogs. Thousands of dogs have died from rawhide, having swallowed the hide after it has become soft and mushy, only to cause stomach and intestinal blockage. A new rawhide product on the market has finally solved the problem of rawhide: molded Roar-Hide® from Nylabone. These are composed of processed, cut up, and melted American

A new rawhide product has finally solved the problems of rawhide: Roar-Hide® by Nylabone®. These dog-safe devices smell and taste like rawhide but don't break up.

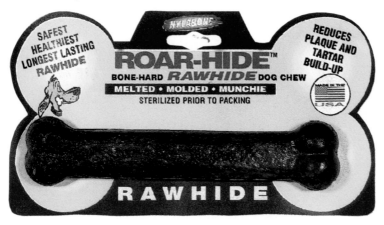

rawhide injected into your dog's favorite shape: a dog bone. These dog-safe devices smell and taste like rawhide but don't break up. The ridges on the bones help to fight tartar build-up on the teeth and they last ten times longer than the usual rawhide chews.

As your dog ages, professional examination and cleaning should become more frequent. The mouth should be inspected at least once a year. Your veterinarian may recommend visits every six months. In the geriatric patient, organs such as the heart, liver, and kidneys do not function as well as when they were young. Your veterinarian will probably want to test these organs' functions prior to using general anesthesia for dental cleaning.

The Gumabone® Frisbee® * has a dog bone molded on the top, which makes it easier for your Cocker Spaniel to pick up. *The trademark Frisbee is used under license from Mattel, Inc. California, U.S.A.

If your dog is a good chewer and you work closely with your veterinarian, your dog can keep all of its teeth all of its life. However, as your dog ages, his sense of smell, sight, and taste will diminish. He may not have the desire to chase, trap or chew his toys. He will also not have the energy to chew for long periods, as arthritis and periodontal disease make chewing painful. This will leave you with more responsibility for keeping his teeth clean and healthy. The dog that would not let you brush his teeth at one year of age, may let you brush his teeth now that he is ten years old.

If you train your dog with good chewing habits as a puppy, he will have healthier teeth throughout his life.

Teach your puppy constructive chewing habits by providing him with an array of Nylabone® products.

HEALTH CARE for Your Cocker Spaniel

Veterinary medicine has become far more sophisticated than what was available to our ancestors. This can be attributed to the increase in household pets and consequently the demand for better care for them. Also human medicine has become far more complex. Today diagnostic testing in veterinary medicine parallels human diagnostics. Because of better technology we can expect our pets to live healthier lives thereby increasing their life spans.

THE FIRST CHECK UP

With all the love and devotion your Cocker Spaniel offers you, no amount of love and care can be too great.

You will want to take your new puppy/dog in for its first check up within 48 to 72 hours after acquiring it. Many breeders strongly recommend this check up and so do the humane shelters. A puppy/dog can appear healthy but it may have a serious problem that is not apparent to the layman. Most pets have some type of a minor flaw that may never cause a real problem.

Unfortunately if he/she should have a serious problem, you will want to consider the consequences of keeping the pet and the attachments that will be formed, which may be broken prematurely. Keep in mind there are many healthy dogs looking for good homes.

This first check up is a good time to establish yourself with the veterinarian and learn the office policy regarding their hours and how they handle emergencies. Usually the breeder or another conscientious pet owner is a good reference for locating a capable veterinarian. You should be aware that not all veterinarians give the same quality of service. Please do not make your selection on the least expensive clinic, as they may be short changing your pet. There is the possibility that eventually it will cost you more due to improper diagnosis, treatment, etc. If you are selecting a new veterinarian, feel free to ask for a tour of the clinic. You should inquire about making an

appointment for a tour since all clinics are working clinics, and therefore may not be available all day for sightseers. You may worry less if you see where your pet will be spending the day if he ever needs to be hospitalized.

THE PHYSICAL EXAM

Your veterinarian will check your pet's overall condition, which includes listening to the heart; checking the respiration; feeling the abdomen, muscles and joints; checking the mouth, which includes the gum color and signs of gum disease along with plaque buildup; checking the ears for signs of an infection or ear mites; examining the eyes; and, last but not least, checking the condition of the skin and coat.

He should ask you questions regarding your pet's eating and elimination habits and invite you to relay your questions. It is a good idea to prepare a list so as not to forget anything. He should discuss the proper diet and the quantity to be fed. If this should differ from your breeder's recommendation, then you should convey to him the breeder's choice and see if he approves. If he recommends changing the diet, then this should be done over a few days so as not to cause a gastrointestinal upset. It is customary to take in a fresh stool sample (just a small amount) for a test for intestinal parasites. It must be fresh, preferably within 12 hours, since the eggs hatch quickly and after hatching will not be observed under the microscope. If your pet

When visiting the veterinarian, it is customary to take a stool sample to test for intestinal parasites, such as roundworms. Courtesy of Merck AgVet.

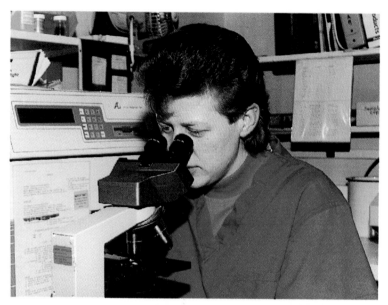

Laboratory tests are studied by highly trained veterinary technicians. Most tests are performed right in your own veterinarian's office.

isn't obliging then, usually the technician can take one in the clinic.

IMMUNIZATIONS

It is important that you take your puppy/dog's vaccination record with you on your first visit. In case of a puppy, presumably the breeder has seen to the vaccinations up to the time you acquired custody. Veterinarians differ in their vaccination protocol. It is not unusual for your puppy to have received vaccinations for distemper, hepatitis, leptospirosis, parvovirus and parainfluenza every two to three weeks from the age of five or six weeks. Usually this is a combined injection and is typically called the DHLPP. The DHLPP is given through at least 12 to 14 weeks of age, and it is customary to continue with another parvovirus vaccine at 16 to 18 weeks. You may wonder why so many immunizations are necessary. No one knows for sure when the puppy's maternal antibodies are gone, although it is customarily accepted that distemper antibodies are gone by 12 weeks. Usually parvovirus antibodies are gone by 16 to 18 weeks of age.

However, it is possible for the maternal antibodies to be gone at a much earlier age or even a later age. Therefore immunizations are started at an early age. The vaccine will not give immunity as long as there are maternal antibodies.

The rabies vaccination is given at three or six months of age depending on your local laws. A vaccine for bordetella (kennel cough) is advisable and can be given anytime from the age of five weeks. The coronavirus is not commonly given unless there is a problem locally. The Lyme vaccine is necessary in endemic areas. Lyme disease has been reported in 47 states.

Distemper

This is virtually an incurable disease. If the dog recovers, he is subject to severe nervous disorders. The virus attacks every tissue in the body and resembles a bad cold with a fever. It can cause a runny nose and eyes and cause gastrointestinal disorders, including a poor appetite, vomiting and diarrhea. The virus is carried by raccoons, foxes, wolves, mink and other dogs. Unvaccinated youngsters and senior citizens are

Although no one knows for sure when puppies' maternal antibodies are gone, it is usually between 12 to 18 weeks of age. Therefore immunizations should be started early on.

140

very susceptible. This is still a common disease.

Hepatitis

This is a virus that is most serious in very young dogs. It is spread by contact with an infected animal or its stool or urine. The virus affects the liver and kidneys and is characterized by high fever, depression and lack of appetite. Recovered animals may be afflicted with chronic illnesses.

Leptospirosis

This is a bacterial disease transmitted by contact with the urine of an infected dog, rat or other wildlife. It produces severe symptoms of fever, depression, jaundice and internal bleeding and was fatal before the vaccine was developed. Recovered dogs can be carriers, and the disease can be transmitted from dogs to humans.

The deer tick is the main culprit responsible for Lyme disease. The Lyme vaccine is necessary in endemic areas.

Parvovirus

This was first noted in the late 1970s and is still a fatal disease. However, with proper vaccinations, early diagnosis and prompt treatment, it is a manageable disease. It attacks the bone marrow and intestinal tract. The symptoms include depression, loss of appetite, vomiting, diarrhea and collapse. Immediate medical attention is of the essence.

Rabies

This is shed in the saliva and is carried by raccoons, skunks, foxes, other dogs and cats. It attacks nerve tissue, resulting in paralysis and death. Rabies can be transmitted to people and is virtually always fatal. This disease is reappearing in the suburbs.

Bordetella (Kennel Cough)

The symptoms are coughing, sneezing, hacking and

retching accompanied by nasal discharge usually lasting from a few days to several weeks. There are several disease-producing organisms responsible for this disease. The present vaccines are helpful but do not protect for all the strains. It usually is not life threatening but in some instances it can progress to a serious bronchopneumonia. The disease is highly contagious. The vaccination should be given routinely for dogs that come in contact with other dogs, such as through boarding, training class or visits to the groomer.

Coronavirus

This is usually self limiting and not life threatening. It was first noted in the late '70s about a year before parvovirus. The virus produces a yellow/brown stool and there may be depression, vomiting and diarrhea.

Lyme Disease

This was first diagnosed in the United States in 1976 in Lyme, CT in people who lived in close proximity to the deer tick. Symptoms may include acute lameness, fever, swelling of joints and loss of appetite. Your veterinarian can advise you if you live in an endemic area.

After your puppy has completed his puppy vaccinations, you will continue to booster the DHLPP once a year. It is customary to booster the rabies one year after the first vaccine and then, depending on where you live, it should be boostered every year or every three years. This depends on your local laws. The Lyme and corona vaccines are boostered annually and it is recommended that the bordetella be boostered every six to eight months.

ANNUAL VISIT

I would like to impress the importance of the annual check up, which would include the booster vaccinations, check for intestinal parasites and test for heartworm. Today in our very busy world it is rush, rush and see "how much you can get for how little." Unbelievably, some non-veterinary businesses have entered into the vaccination business. More harm than good can come to your dog through improper vaccinations, possibly from inferior vaccines and/or the wrong schedule. More than likely you truly care about your companion dog and over the years you have devoted much time and expense to his well being. Perhaps you are unaware that a vaccination is not just a vaccination. There is more involved. Please, please follow through with regular physical examinations. It is so important for your veterinarian to know your dog and this is especially true during middle age through the geriatric years. More than likely your older dog will require more than one physical a year. The annual physical is good preventive medicine. Through early diagnosis and subsequent treatment your dog can maintain a longer and better quality of life.

It is important to follow through with your Cocker Spaniel's regular examinations, especially during middle age through the geriatric years.

INTESTINAL PARASITES

Hookworms

These are almost microscopic intestinal worms that can cause anemia and therefore serious problems, including death, in young puppies. Hookworms can be transmitted to humans through penetration of the skin. Puppies may be born with them.

Roundworms

These are spaghetti-like worms that can cause a potbellied appearance and dull coat along with more severe symptoms, such as vomiting, diarrhea and coughing. Puppies acquire these while in the mother's uterus and through lactation. Both hookworms and roundworms may be acquired through ingestion.

Whipworms

These have a three-month life cycle and are not acquired through the dam. They cause intermittent diarrhea usually with mucus. Whipworms are possibly the most difficult worm to eradicate. Their eggs are very resistant to most environmental factors and can last for years until the proper conditions enable them to mature. Whipworms are seldom seen in the stool.

Intestinal parasites are more prevalent in some areas than others. Climate, soil and contamination are big factors contributing to the incidence of intestinal parasites. Eggs are passed in the stool, lay on the ground and then become infective in a certain number of days. Each of the above worms has a different life cycle. Your best chance of becoming and remaining worm-free is to always pooper-scoop your yard. A fenced-in yard keeps stray dogs out, which is certainly helpful.

Whipworms are possibly the most difficult worm to eradicate. They cause intermittent diarrhea usually with mucus. Courtesy of Merck AgVet.

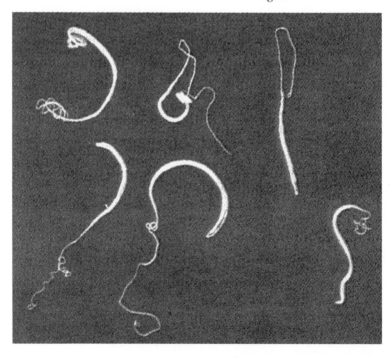

I would recommend having a fecal examination on your dog twice a year or more often if there is a problem. If your dog has a positive fecal sample, then he will be given the appropriate medication and you will be asked to bring back another stool sample in a certain period of time (depending on the type of worm) and then be rewormed. This process goes on until he has at least two negative samples. The different types of worms require different medications. You will be wasting your money and doing your dog an injustice by buying over-the-counter medication without first consulting your veterinarian.

OTHER INTERNAL PARASITES

Coccidiosis and Giardiasis

These protozoal infections usually affect puppies, especially in places where large numbers of puppies are brought together. Older dogs may harbor these infections but do not show signs unless they are stressed. Symptoms include diarrhea, weight loss and lack of appetite. These infections are not always apparent in the fecal examination.

Dirofilaria—adult worms in heart of a dog. It is possible for a dog to be infected with any number of worms from one to a hundred. Courtesy of Merck AgVet.

Tapeworms

Seldom apparent on fecal floatation, they are diagnosed frequently as rice-like segments around the dog's anus and the base of the tail. Tapeworms are long, flat and ribbon like, sometimes several feet in length, and made up of many segments about five-eighths of an inch long. The two most common types of tapeworms found in the dog are:

(1) First the larval form of the flea tapeworm parasite must mature in an intermediate host, the flea, before it can become infective. Your dog acquires this by ingesting the flea through licking and chewing.

(2) Rabbits, rodents and certain large game animals serve

as intermediate hosts for other species of tapeworms. If your dog should eat one of these infected hosts, then he can acquire tapeworms.

HEARTWORM DISEASE

This is a worm that resides in the heart and adjacent blood vessels of the lung that produces microfilaria, which circulate in the bloodstream. It is possible for a dog to be infected with any number of worms from one to a hundred that can be 6 to 14 inches long. It is a life-threatening disease, expensive to treat and easily prevented. Depending on where you live, your veterinarian may recommend a preventive year-round and either an annual or semiannual blood test. The most common preventive is given once a month.

EXTERNAL PARASITES

Fleas

These pests are not only the dog's worst enemy but also enemy to the owner's pocketbook. Preventing is less expensive than treating, but regardless I think we'd prefer to spend our money

The cat flea is the most common flea of both dogs and cats. Courtesy of Fleabusters, Rx for Fleas, Inc., Ft. Lauderdale, Florida.

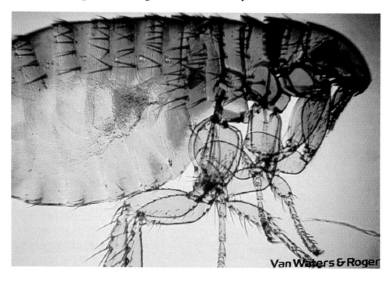

Van Waters & Roger

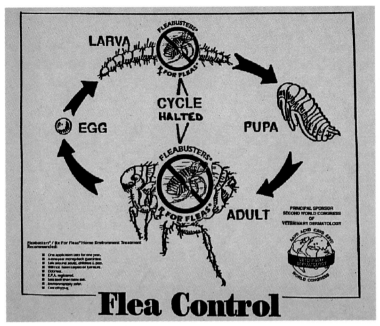

Flea Control

The life cycle of a flea takes 21 to 28 days under ideal conditions. Courtesy of Fleabusters, Rx for Fleas, Inc., Ft. Lauderdale, Florida.

elsewhere. I would guess that the majority of our dogs are allergic to the bite of a flea, and in many cases it only takes one flea bite. The protein in the flea's saliva is the culprit. Allergic dogs have a reaction, which usually results in a "hot spot." More than likely such a reaction will involve a trip to the veterinarian for treatment. Yes, prevention is less expensive. Fortunately today there are several good products available.

If there is a flea infestation, no one product is going to correct the problem. Not only will the dog require treatment so will the environment. In general flea collars are not very effective although there is now available an "egg" collar that will kill the eggs on the dog. Dips are the most economical but they are messy. There are some effective shampoos and treatments available through pet shops and veterinarians. An oral tablet arrived on the American market in 1995 and was popular in Europe the previous year. It sterilizes the female flea but will not kill adult fleas. Therefore the tablet, which is given monthly, will decrease the flea population but is not a "cure-all." Those dogs that suffer from flea-bite allergy will still be subjected to the bite of the flea. Another popular parasiticide is permethrin, which is applied to the back of the dog in one or two places depending on the dog's weight. This product works as a repellent causing the flea to get "hot feet" and jump off. Do not confuse this product with some of the organophosphates that are also applied to the dog's back.

Some products are not usable on young puppies. Treating fleas should be done under your veterinarian's guidance. Frequently it is necessary to combine products and the layman does not have the knowledge regarding possible toxicities. It is hard to believe but there are a few dogs that do have a natural resistance to fleas. Nevertheless it would be wise to treat all pets at the same time. Don't forget your cats. Cats just love to prowl the neighborhood and consequently return with unwanted guests.

An Elizabethan collar is used to keep dogs from licking sensitive or itchy areas.

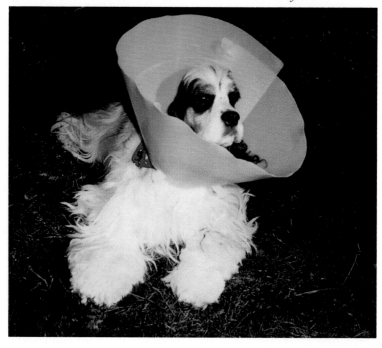

Adult fleas live on the dog but their eggs drop off the dog into the environment. There they go through four larval stages before reaching adulthood, and thereby are able to jump back on the poor unsuspecting dog. The cycle resumes and takes between 21 to 28 days under ideal conditions. There are environmental products available that will kill both the adult fleas and the larvae.

Ticks

Ticks carry Rocky Mountain Spotted Fever, Lyme disease and can cause tick paralysis. They should be removed with tweezers, trying to pull out the head. The jaws carry disease. There is a tick preventive collar that does an excellent job. The ticks automatically back out on those dogs wearing collars.

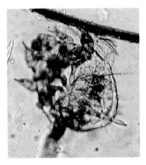

Sarcoptes are highly contagious to other dogs and to humans, although they do not live long on humans. They cause intense itching.

Sarcoptic Mange

This is a mite that is difficult to find on skin scrapings. The pinnal reflex is a good indicator of this disease. Rub the ends of the pinna (ear) together and the dog will start scratching with his foot. Sarcoptes are highly contagious to other dogs and to humans although they do not live long on humans. They cause intense itching.

Demodectic Mange

This is a mite that is passed from the dam to her puppies. It affects youngsters age three to ten months. Diagnosis is confirmed by skin scraping. Small areas of alopecia around the eyes, lips and/or forelegs become visible. There is little itching unless there is a secondary bacterial infection. Some breeds are afflicted more than others.

Cheyletiella

This causes intense itching and is diagnosed by skin

scraping. It lives in the outer layers of the skin of dogs, cats, rabbits and humans. Yellow-gray scales may be found on the back and the rump, top of the head and the nose.

TO BREED OR NOT TO BREED

More than likely your breeder has requested that you have your puppy neutered or spayed. Your breeder's request is based on what is healthiest for your dog and what is most beneficial for your breed. Experienced and conscientious breeders devote many years into developing a bloodline. In order to do this, he makes every effort to plan each breeding in regard to conformation, temperament and health. This type of breeder does his best to perform the necessary testing (i.e., OFA, CERF, testing for inherited blood disorders, thyroid, etc.). Testing is expensive and sometimes very disheartening when a favorite dog doesn't pass his health tests. The health history pertains not only to the breeding stock but to the immediate ancestors. Reputable breeders do not want their offspring to be bred indiscriminately. Therefore you may be asked to neuter or spay your puppy. Of course there is always the exception, and your breeder may agree to let you breed your dog under his direct supervision. This is an important concept. More and more effort is being made to breed healthier dogs.

Spay/Neuter

There are numerous benefits of performing this surgery at six months of age. Unspayed females are subject to mammary and ovarian cancer. In order to prevent mammary cancer she must be spayed prior to her first heat cycle. Later in life, an unspayed female may develop a pyometra (an infected uterus), which is definitely life threatening.

Spaying is performed under a general anesthetic and is easy on the young dog. As you might expect it is a little harder on the older dog, but that is no reason to deny her the surgery. The surgery removes the ovaries and uterus. It is important to remove all the ovarian tissue. If some is left behind, she could remain attractive to males. In order to view the ovaries, a reasonably long incision is necessary. An ovariohysterectomy is considered major surgery.

Neutering the male at a young age will inhibit some characteristic male behavior that owners frown upon. I have found my boys will not hike their legs and mark territory if they are neutered at six months of age. Also neutering at a young age has hormonal benefits, lessening the chance of hormonal aggressiveness.

Surgery involves removing the testicles but leaving the scrotum. If there should be a retained testicle, then he definitely needs to be neutered before the age of two or three years. Retained testicles can develop into cancer. Unneutered males are at risk for testicular cancer, perineal fistulas, perianal tumors and fistulas and prostatic disease.

Intact males and females are prone to housebreaking accidents. Females urinate frequently before, during and after heat cycles, and males tend to mark territory if there is a female in heat. Males may show the same behavior if there is a visiting dog or guests.

Surgery involves a sterile operating procedure equivalent to human surgery. The incision site is shaved, surgically scrubbed and draped. The veterinarian wears a sterile surgical gown, cap, mask and gloves. Anesthesia should be monitored by a registered technician. It is customary for the veterinarian to recommend a pre-anesthetic blood screening, looking for metabolic problems and a ECG rhythm strip to check for normal heart function. Today anesthetics are equal to human anesthetics, which enables your dog to walk out of the clinic the same day as surgery.

Some folks worry about their dog gaining weight after being neutered or spayed. This is usually not the case. It is true that some dogs may be less active so they could develop a problem, but my own dogs are just as active as they were before surgery. I have a hard time keeping weight on them. However, if your dog should begin to gain, then you need to decrease his food and see to it that he gets a little more exercise.

IDENTIFICATION and Finding the Lost Dog

There are several ways of identifying your dog. The old standby is a collar with dog license, rabies, and ID tags. Unfortunately collars have a way of being separated from the dog and tags fall off. I am not suggesting you shouldn't use a collar and tags. If they stay intact and on the dog, they are the quickest way of identification.

For several years owners have been tattooing their dogs. Some tattoos use a number with a registry. Here lies the problem because there are several registries to check. If you wish to tattoo, use your social security number. The humane shelters have the means to trace it. It is usually done on the inside of the rear thigh. The area is first shaved and numbed. There is no pain, although a few dogs do not like the buzzing sound. Occasionally tattooing is not legible and needs to be redone.

The newest method of identification is microchipping. The microchip is a computer chip that is no larger than a grain of rice. The veterinarian implants it by injection between the shoulder blades. The dog feels no discomfort. If your dog is lost and picked up by the humane society, they can trace you by scanning the microchip, which has its own code. Microchip scanners are friendly to other brands of microchips and their registries. The microchip comes with a dog tag saying the dog is microchipped. It is the safest way of identifying your dog.

FINDING THE LOST DOG

I am sure you will agree with me that there would be little worse than losing your dog. Responsible pet owners rarely lose their dogs. They do not let their dogs run free because they don't want harm to come to them. Not only that but in most, if not all, states there is a leash law.

Beware of fenced-in yards. They can be a hazard. Dogs find ways to escape either over or under the fence. Another fast exit is through the gate that perhaps the neighbor's child left unlocked.

Below is a list that hopefully will be of help to you if you need it. Remember don't give up, keep looking. Your dog is worth your efforts.

1. Contact your neighbors and put flyers with a photo on it in their mailboxes. Information you should include would be the dog's name, breed, sex, color, age, source of identification, when your dog was last seen and where, and your name and phone numbers. It may be helpful to say the dog needs medical care. Offer a *reward*.

2. Check all local shelters daily. It is also possible for your dog to be picked up away from home and end up in an out-of-the-way shelter. Check these too. Go in person. It is not good enough to call. Most shelters are limited on the time they can hold dogs then they are put up for adoption or euthanized. There is the possibility that your dog will not make it to the shelter for several days. Your dog could have been wandering or someone may have tried to keep him.

The newest form of identification is microchipping. If your dog is lost and picked up by the humane society, they can trace you by scanning the microchip.

3. Notify all local veterinarians. Call and send flyers.

4. Call your breeder. Frequently breeders are contacted when one of their breed is found.

5. Contact the rescue group for your breed.

6. Contact local schools—children may have seen your dog.

7. Post flyers at the schools, groceries, gas stations, convenience stores, veterinary clinics, groomers and any other place that will allow them.

8. Advertise in the newspaper.

9. Advertise on the radio.

Traveling with Your Dog

The earlier you start traveling with your new puppy or dog, the better. He needs to become accustomed to traveling. However, some dogs are nervous riders and become carsick easily. It is helpful if he starts with an empty stomach. Do not despair, as it will go better if you continue taking him with you on short fun rides. How would you feel if every time you rode in the car you stopped at the doctor's for an injection? You would soon dread that nasty car. Older dogs that tend to get carsick may have more of a problem adjusting to traveling. Those dogs that are having a serious problem may benefit from some medication prescribed by the veterinarian.

Do give your dog a chance to relieve himself before getting into the car. It is a good idea to be prepared for a clean up with a leash, paper towels, bag and terry cloth towel.

The safest place for your dog is in a fiberglass crate, although close confinement can promote carsickness in some dogs. If your dog is nervous you can try letting him ride on the seat next to you or in someone's lap.

An alternative to the crate would be to use a car harness made for dogs and/or a safety strap attached to the harness or collar. Whatever you do, do not let your dog ride in the back of a pickup truck unless he is securely tied on a very short lead. I've seen trucks stop quickly and, even though the dog was tied, it fell out and was dragged.

I do occasionally let my dogs ride loose with me because I really enjoy their companionship, but in all honesty they are safer in their crates. I have a friend whose van rolled in an accident but his dogs, in their fiberglass crates, were not injured nor did they escape. Another advantage of the crate is that it is a safe place to leave him if you need to run into the store. Otherwise you wouldn't be able to leave the windows down. Keep in mind that while many dogs are overly protective in their crates, this may not be enough to deter dognappers. In some states it is against the law to leave a dog in the car unattended.

Never leave a dog loose in the car wearing a collar and leash.

You shouldn't let your Cocker Spaniel put his head out of the car window when traveling. Debris could blow in his eyes.

I have known more than one dog that has killed himself by hanging. Do not let him put his head out an open window. Foreign debris can be blown into his eyes. When leaving your dog unattended in a car, consider the temperature. It can take less than five minutes to reach temperatures over 100 degrees Fahrenheit.

TRIPS

Perhaps you are taking a trip. Give consideration to what is best for your dog–traveling with you or boarding. When traveling by car, van or motor home, you need to think ahead about locking your vehicle. In all probability you have many valuables in the car and do not wish to leave it unlocked. Perhaps most valuable and not replaceable is your dog. Give thought to securing your vehicle and providing adequate ventilation for him. Another consideration for you when traveling with your dog is medical problems that may arise and little inconveniences, such as exposure to external parasites. Some areas of the country are quite flea infested. You may want to carry flea spray with you. This is even a good idea when staying in motels. Quite possibly you are not the only occupant of the room.

Unbelievably many motels and even hotels do allow canine guests, even some very first-class ones. Gaines Pet Foods Corporation publishes *Touring With Towser*, a directory of domestic hotels and motels that accommodate guests with dogs. Their address is Gaines TWT, PO Box 5700, Kankakee, IL, 60902. I would recommend you call ahead to any motel that you may be considering and see if they accept pets. Sometimes it is necessary to pay a deposit against room damage. Of course you are more likely to gain accommodations for a small dog than a large dog. Also the management feels reassured when you mention that your dog will be crated. Since my dogs tend to bark when I leave the room, I leave the TV on nearly full blast to deaden the noises outside that tend to encourage my dogs to bark. If you do travel with your dog, take along plenty of baggies so that you can clean up after him. When we all do our share in cleaning up, we make it possible for motels to continue accepting our pets. As a matter of fact, you should practice cleaning up everywhere you take your dog.

Depending on where you are traveling, you may need an up-to-date health certificate issued by your veterinarian. It is good policy to take along your dog's medical information, which would include the name, address and phone number of your veterinarian, vaccination record, rabies certificate, and any medication he is taking.

AIR TRAVEL

When traveling by air, you need to contact the airlines to check their policy. Usually you have to make arrangements up to a couple of weeks in advance for traveling with your dog. The airlines require your dog to travel in an airline approved fiberglass crate. Usually these can be purchased through the airlines but they are also readily available in most pet-supply stores. If your dog is not accustomed to a crate, then it is a good idea to get him acclimated to it before your trip. The day of the actual trip you should withhold water about one hour ahead of departure and no food for about 12 hours. The airlines generally have temperature restrictions, which do not allow pets to travel if it is either too cold or too hot. Frequently these restrictions are based on the temperatures at the departure and arrival airports. It's best to inquire about a health certificate. These usually need to be issued within ten days of departure. You should arrange for non-stop, direct flights and if a commuter plane should be involved, check to see if it will carry dogs. Some don't. The Humane Society of the United States has put together a tip sheet for airline traveling. You can receive a copy by sending a self-addressed stamped envelope to:

The Humane Society of the United States
Tip Sheet
2100 L Street NW
Washington, DC 20037.

Regulations differ for traveling outside of the country and are sometimes changed without notice. Well in advance you need to write or call the appropriate consulate or agricultural department for instructions. Some countries have lengthy quarantines (six months), and countries differ in their rabies vaccination requirements. For instance, it may have to be given at least 30 days ahead of your departure.

Do make sure your dog is wearing proper identification. You never know when you might be in an accident and separated from your dog. Or your dog could be frightened and somehow manage to escape and run away. When I travel, my dogs wear collars with engraved nameplates with my name, phone number and city.

Another suggestion would be to carry in-case-of-emergency instructions. These would include the address and phone number of a relative or friend, your veterinarian's name, address and phone number, and your dog's medical information.

BOARDING KENNELS

Perhaps you have decided that you need to board your dog. Your veterinarian can recommend a good boarding facility or possibly a pet sitter that will come to your house. It is customary for the boarding kennel to ask for proof of vaccination for the DHLPP, rabies and bordetella vaccine. The bordetella should have been given within six months of boarding. This is for your protection. If they do not ask for this proof I would not board at their kennel. Ask about flea control. Those dogs that suffer flea-bite allergy can get in trouble at a boarding kennel. Unfortunately boarding kennels are limited on how much they are able to do.

For more information on pet sitting, contact NAPPS: National Association of Professional Pet Sitters
1200 G Street, NW
Suite 760
Washington, DC 20005.

Our clinic has technicians that pet sit and technicians that board clinic patients in their homes. This may be an alternative for you. Ask your veterinarian if they have an employee that can help you. There is a definite advantage of having a technician care for your dog, especially if your dog is on medication or is a senior citizen.

You can write for a copy of *Traveling With Your Pet* from ASPCA, Education Department, 441 E. 92nd Street, New York, NY 10128.

Crates are a safe way for your dog to travel. The fiberglass crates are safest but the metal crates allow more air.

SUGGESTED READING

TS-148
The World of the
Cocker Spaniel
624 pages, over
1500 color photos.

TW-141
The Proper Care of
Cocker Spaniels
264 pages, over 240
color photos.

H-1034
The Book of the Cocker
Spaniel
334 pages.

TS-196
Cocker Spaniel
352 pages, over 400
color photos.

TS-205
Successful Dog
Training
160 pages, 130
color photos.

TS-258
Training Your Dog
For Sports and
Other Activities
160 pages, over 200
color photos.

TS-252
Dog Behavior and
Training
288 pages, nearly 200
color photos.

TS-249
Skin & Coat Care for
Your Dog
224 pages, 300 color
photos.

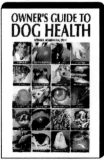

TS-214
Owner's Guide to Dog
Health
300 pages, 150 color
photos.

INDEX